We Are Civic Media

We Are Civic Media

EDITED BY

Sangita Shresthova
Dan Sinker
Pratik Nyaupane
Sophie Madej

AND

Colin Maclay

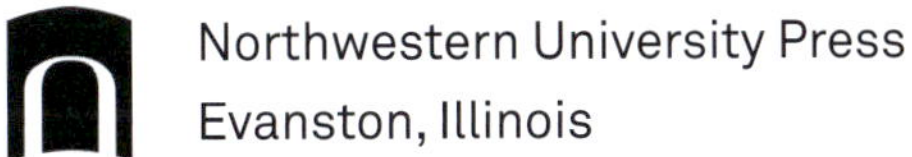
Northwestern University Press
Evanston, Illinois

Northwestern University Press
www.nupress.northwestern.edu

The quote from bell hooks that appears on page 126 in "Dream, Rest, Play: Reflections on Designing Liberated Spaces for Black Women" is from *Sisters of the Yam: Black Women and Self-Recovery* (Routledge, 2014). Reproduced with permission of the Licensor through PLSclear.

The editors recognize the John D. and Catherine T. MacArthur Foundation for their visionary and unwavering support, which has been fundamental to creating and sustaining the USC Civic Media Fellowship, and also to ensuring this book later be released as an Open Access publication.

The editors deeply appreciate the many contributions of our colleagues and institutional homes, including the Annenberg Innovation Lab, the Annenberg School for Communication and Journalism, and the University of Southern California.

Printed in Canada

10 9 8 7 6 5 4 3 2 1

ISBN 978-0-8101-4906-9 (paper)
ISBN 978-0-8101-4907-6 (ebook)

Cataloging-in-Publication Data are available from the Library of Congress.

We dedicate this work to the vibrant people and organizations who encourage, practice, and engage with civic media—past, present, and future!

Contents

Design and Care

Claiming and Reclaiming

Editors' Introduction

The Year is 2084. A major revolution has taken place on Earth after decades of recovering from what the generation before called "the digital apocalypse." Mass mining for electronics, depleted natural resources, and biased technologies pitted humans against each other. The result: a cyber-war that led to governments around the world shutting down the internet for good. For 30 years, there was a digital dark age where the systems that depended on personal data and social media platforms—the systems that shaped the early 2000s—were gone . . .

A new generation has emerged, determined not to repeat the mistakes of those before. Hungry to rebuild, they started from what was needed, what they feared, and what they dreamed. They built slowly, starting small—neighborhood by neighborhood. The future defined itself in a merging of nature and technology. What was created holds beauty in every corner, genuine in every way. Today's people believe this place to be The Marvel.

—Civic Media fellows, *Once Upon a Tech*

Of course, we don't live in 2084. The story of The Marvel comes not from the future but from *Once Upon a Tech*, a 2021 illustrated sci-fi collection of stories set in an imagined future world. The postapocalyptic world of The Marvel is one where all media infrastructures that we associate with the digital age have been decimated or permanently altered, and yet this is not a world without hope. In The Marvel, the inhabitants have learned from the mistakes of the past and are committed to finding new ways to live. From an escape from a faulty artificial intelligence (AI) lifeguard to relearning how to have real-time face-to-face conversations that aren't monitored by robots, the stories in this collection imagine a radically different future that isn't just about surviving another apocalypse. The focus is on building a future grounded in radical social equity and humanity.

The stories in *Once Upon a Tech* were created by artists, creators, storytellers, and organizers affiliated with the Civic Media Fellowship at the University of Southern

California and provide a testament to the authors' dedication to pushing back on accepted definitions and approaches to media creation and social change. This commitment is not just a professional obligation but a deeply personal one, resonating in the narrative woven throughout this speculative fiction. The storylines fellows created are not mere flights of fancy. Rather, they mirror the authors' engagement with present-day issues, reflecting a collective vision that prioritizes human agency and connection over technological dominance. This intermingling of storytelling with community, social mobilization, and imagination is what we call civic media.

A world without media technologies is impossible to imagine. We could not write this book, attend school, or keep up with our closest friends and families without the screens that we cannot escape and the bright and shiny tools on them. And yet with technologies, practices, business models, market structures, and regulations often in tension with personal well-being and societal goals, our reliance upon and prioritization of digital media can also be troubling.

Although the techno-utopianism of the past envisioned that media technologies would level the playing field, the concentration of attention, power, wealth, and assets has created dystopian dynamics closer to *Once Upon a Tech* than many realize. The rise of social media has concentrated online discourse largely into the hands of a single corporation, Meta (which owns Facebook, Instagram, and WhatsApp); two companies, Google and Apple, control our phones; Google maintains a chokehold on web searches, web video (via YouTube), and advertising; and Microsoft continues its decades-long dominance in operating systems. The rise of AI presents opportunities to change these dynamics, but it may wreak even more profound changes across various industries, potentially transforming everything from job markets to personal privacy and governance. Indeed, these same companies acquire potentially disruptive start-up companies and technologies to avoid any threat and cement control and are endeavoring to be leaders in AI. Severely limited competition and regulation mean that these companies—and all their inbuilt technological and operational biases—face little pressure to better serve all people, especially those from diverse and marginalized communities.

We don't live in The Marvel; we live in the now. Indeed, we don't need a fictional digital apocalypse to know that the way we consume, interact with, and make media to connect with each other needs to change. From mainstream media that ignores, misunderstands, and mischaracterizes the experiences of so many communities to social platforms whose quest for attention and revenue rewards performance and polarization rather than usefulness and connection, our media and technology infrastructures are serving people and society poorly. And while many of us recognize that most people don't feel like they have the ability to change it—or the luxury to opt out—the challenges surrounding us, from immigration and education to criminal justice reform and climate change, grow more daunting every day.

Our current moment is formidable but also has a few hopeful and disruptive elements. In a world of incredibly powerful technologies and ever more urgent social issues, finding a voice and listening to each other might seem impossible. And yet, against long odds, this period has also been significantly defined by emergent and sustained grassroots movements, independent media, and labor organizing, driven by creative individuals and groups working to spread the stories, visions, strategies, and dreams that are often overlooked in the dominant narratives, at least initially. At a time when things seem especially grim—both in spite and because of it—our desire to connect, create, and act is playing a pivotal role in shaping societal narratives, influencing policymaking, and empowering communities.

Every act of genuine creation is an act of resistance that takes us one step closer to rewriting the narratives about ourselves, our lives, and our present. Civic media practice has a vision for the future, recognizes the present, and pays active attention to the past (and ancestors in particular). Its power is the journey and the convening of minds, bodies, and tools—creating stories—with an intention to drive progress. Just as the civic media makers in *We Are Civic Media* know that the cyber war of *Once Upon a Tech* hasn't happened, we know that the future isn't fixed, that it's open for the writing. We know that the future will be defined by those who dare to build it.

Civic media isn't a thing, but a who, how, and why. It is embodied by the organizers, the content creators, the artists, the storytellers, and the people in our homes and communities who craft and make media. The contributors in this collection are part of a growing network of multifaceted, multidisciplinary, and generally uncategorizable thinkers and practitioners who are leading and redefining how we think and approach civic media as they center people and communities and their stories that connect and mobilize around issues of shared concern and urge us to focus on participation and relationships.

The practices and values we connect to civic media are very important in an era of rising authoritarianism and declining trust in public institutions. Indeed, civic media and civic media creators help us stand up and hold power to account. They provide invaluable guidance on how emerging technologies can be designed, implemented, and regulated to support individual and collective well-being. Features such as interconnection, authenticity, trust, and the reciprocity motive offer a refreshing contrast to media driven by unfettered capitalism and political self-interest and their shared potential to subvert community and democracy. Put bluntly, paying attention to those who make and engage with civic media is not just important; it is imperative to advancing equity, justice, and ultimately democracy.

We know that the future will be defined by those who dare to build it.

About the Civic Media Fellowship

Conceived in 2018 with support from the John D. and Catherine T. MacArthur Foundation, the Civic Media Fellowship engages artists, creators, storytellers, organizers, and others working at the intersections of media, technology, culture, and social change. Based at the University of Southern California, the fellowship offers programming and other support to fellows for a period of nine months with the vision of nurturing a sustained and expansive peer-based supportive network.

The fellowship flows in three overlapping arcs that seek to answer the following questions: Why are we here? What can we do? And where will we go? Ever attentive to balancing commitments and exploration, we engage in conversations and activities that might not seem directly related to our work, with the understanding that these experiences will yield valuable insights and benefits in the long run.

Past activities that correlated with these arcs included sharing short visual storytelling presentations to narrate personal journeys and identify common experiences and values and engaging in fellow-led workshops on innovative topics. Some of these shared elements of the fellows' methods of action, like Afrofuturist world-building, speculative story making, and collective songwriting. Others shared practices that held deep connections to their worldviews, such as fermentation techniques, Daoist medicine, goat milking, making protest valentines, and natural dyeing using elements from one's pantry or bodega. Still others invited everyone to examine their own practice from a new perspective, such as *ikigai*, reclaiming pleasure as an antidote to despair, and taking a career break when your work is your identity.

Above all, the fellowship year is a time that the fellows can use for a range of pursuits, from taking the time to reset and exploring new interests, to reinvigorating their existing practices or embarking on ambitious new endeavors. After the formal program ends, alumni are welcomed to continue as senior fellows and are invited to join in programming, mentoring, program leadership, and virtually all other aspects of community life.

The fellowship was both motivated by, and has reinforced a shared appreciation for, civic media makers and their potential to advance social change for communities who had long been disempowered and otherwise marginalized. Change in traditional media was long overdue, and while digital media seemingly held some promise, civic media makers were clearly onto something that resonated. They were having a meaningful impact and charging ahead, despite facing incredible headwinds fueled by limited resources, invisibility, indifference, antipathy, and more . . . all undergirded by systemic inequities. They were repurposing media, creating powerful cultural strategies, gathering community in safe and brave spaces, and otherwise demonstrating the viability of innovative ideas and practices to raise awareness, deepen understanding, and promote action. In the words of Amber J. Phillips, a fellow, activist, artist, and performer who creates narratives through her lens of being a "fat Black queer femme auntie from the Midwest": "Civic media is creating media with the intention of causing people to take action somewhere in their lives to make themselves or the communities that they exist in better than how they found them."

Civic Media in Broader Context

"Civic media" is not a term that we invented or created, but it does not circulate broadly in media and social change domains. And therein lies both the challenge and the opportunity to embrace the term in this book and beyond. On the one hand, civic media can feel like an abstract concept, beholden to a somewhat obscure lineage whose latest chapter traces its origins to the early 2000s. On the other hand, it presents an opportunity to define it with, for, and in service of civic media practitioners and those who support them.

In fact, most fellows said that they had not heard of civic media before applying to the program. They also did not necessarily see their work as civic media. Some still do not. Their identities and projects span a diverse lexicon, encompassing terms like "social practice," "social impact," and "social justice," as well as "narrative and cultural strategies." Others identify with more specific niches, such as "immersive experiential projects," "cultural architecture," "community building," "storytelling," and "social change initiatives." Some embrace "stuntin' on the opposition," "cultural landscaping," and "base building." "Culture jamming" and "cultural interventions" are part of their repertoire. This rich tapestry of descriptions underscores the multifaceted nature of their endeavors—and the fluid nature of what we call civic media. As one Civic Media fellow poignantly reflected, "I honestly didn't have a term for what I did till I became a part of this fellowship."

While the history of civic media could be seen as spanning centuries, including the use of pamphlets and broadsides that informed and promoted political and social causes, alongside the citizen journalism and civic technology movements of the early 2000s, our attention is on more recent practices and conceptualizations of civic media. The rise of social media invited us to imagine the democratizing potential of using social media for civic engagement. Many were captivated by the promise of what could be, with scholars of civic media describing the ways digital tools could bring together communities, foster dialogue, and even facilitate social change.

Less than a decade later, civic media advocates' optimism had waned significantly. While the affordances of social media were still mentioned in passing (and invaluable in many communities), public attention was now fixated on the creeping polarization of public discourse and the proliferation of misinformation and disinformation. In addition to taking limited action against systemic abuses, the power dynamics inherent in media ownership and control have also emerged as key limiting factors for marginalized groups wanting to use media platforms for social change. The very tools that we hoped might help level the playing field were in fact being used to perpetuate the racial, socioeconomic, and other biases that sustain structural inequity.

Taking these and other concerns into account alongside other trends they had observed as digital media came into its own in the early 2000s, scholars and practitioners made a case for civic media as the collective mediacentric practices that advocate for a "common good."[1] In this context, civic media reflected the variable and uneven changing landscape of media technologies with the potential for these changes to be useful to those advocating for civic engagement and social activism.

An Evolving Definition

Rather than binding ourselves to any fixed definitions, we are guided by the voices and stories of the people who live, breathe, and practice through these diverse forms of media—namely, the fellows and other practitioners in our network. In our discussions, fellows did not shy from pushing back on the term "civic media," pointing out that these two words were coined by others in another era. To some Civic Media fellows—who work across film, visual art, performance, and sound—"civic" is tied to so many other words with roots that are tied to exclusion. Terms such as "civic," "citizen," and "democracy" are indeed leveraged by many within systems to exclude, to silence, and to impose.

We realize that without moral integrity (characterized by a caring attitude) or ethical awareness (being mindful of the impact one's actions have on a broader, sometimes remote, community) as defined by Carrie James in the book *Disconnected*,[2] the practices we connect to civic media may not be genuinely civic. Absent these vital components, the same tools lauded for their civic potential can transform into platforms for intimidation and abuse, silencing dissent and facilitating the spread of hatred, conspiracy theories, and inaccurate information. We clearly need to heed the warnings about the destructive potentials of these practices and the real damage and harm they can do. Even so, strategies used by practitioners and noted by academics in the decade after the turn of the millennium hinted at civic media's possible positive impact, holding out hope that these practices and approaches might still have the power to connect and bolster initiatives aimed at engaging more individuals and enriching the core activities vital for a robust and deep democracy.

To that end, each cohort of Civic Media fellows found ways to define the concept for themselves. In codesigning the fellowship program, we invited diverse speakers such as abolitionist educator and activist Mariame Kaba to share teachings on hope as a discipline; The Nap Ministry founder Tricia Hersey to champion rest as resistance; comedian Kristina Wong, writer and illustrator Jonny Sun, and artist and cultural strategist Favianna Rodriguez to talk about reclaiming narratives; scholar and media producer AJ Christian and award-winning public media producer Juan Devis to explore models for cultural production as community building; chair of the Unicode Emoji Subcommittee Jennifer Daniel to talk about inclusion through our tech ecosystems; and theorist and educator Mandy Harris Williams to question how we use social media.

We also engaged several others in smaller-format conversations, including Black feminist political scientist Cathy Cohen on deviance as resistance, scholar Henry Jenkins on the civic imagination, poet and educator Jamaica Heolimeleikalani Osorio and chef Angela Dimayuga on the role of ancestral memory, research and designer Sasha Costanza-Chock on design justice, law professor Dean Spade on mutual aid, media producer and scholar Caty Borum on the role of comedy in social change, games and civic media scholar Benjamin Stokes on the role of play, and transmedia artist Stephanie Dinkins on equitable and values-grounded technologies. Multihyphenate guests like professor and writer Eve Ewing simply spoke about how to balance "doing it all." Guiding insights in our conversations came from thinkers like writer and activist adrienne maree brown to help frame the term "civic media" with a more radical politics and a more queer and BIPOC lens.

Informed by these and other people, we collectively chose to approach the civic media space through bell hooks's reading of Paulo Freire, where "to have work that promotes one's liberation is such a powerful gift that it does not matter so much if the gift is flawed. Think of the work as water that contains some dirt. Because you are thirsty you are not too proud to extract the dirt and be nourished by the water."

Staying true to the ethos and values of the fellowship, we continue to discuss what we think civic media is and could be. Designer, entrepreneur, and cultural architect Daniel Alejandro Leon-Davis highlighted the role of personal experience, stating, "So much of what we do is actually based on our lived experiences, and there is power in vulnerability." The writer, comedian, and podcaster Akilah Hughes (author of "It's Not Cool to Have a Racist High School Mascot") further broadened the scope, suggesting that civic media "addresses the ills of society" and empowers people to seek change. Ingrid Burrington, a writer and artist, added a layer of connectivity, aiming to make "conduits for getting people to talk to each other" and inspire societal evolution. These insights, and many others, collectively bring into focus an understanding of civic media in which individuals and communities share experiences, nurture connections, and tap personal experiences and narratives to drive social change. Justino Mora, an early practitioner of the use of infographics, memes, and short video clips, whose work is rooted in resistance and change, noted that connecting with other fellows helped him "see what civic media looks like through their eyes." In fact, connecting with others may well be at the heart of our evolving definition of civic media as Tyree Boyd-Pates said, "I now don't feel as alone as I felt as a practitioner of civic media."

Over time, these conversations led us to an idea and a process that we eventually nurtured into the book you hold in your hands today, a collection of personal stories from civic media practitioners that, while not aiming to define the field, seeks to personalize and humanize the diverse approaches and experiences within it.

Who Are "We" in *We Are Civic Media*?

The "we" in this book takes on several meanings. In the broader sense, "we" refers to the Civic Media Fellowship community. This includes the staff, fellows, guests, and other networks that we have connected with over the fellowship's existence. In a more narrow sense, our use of "we" in this introductory chapter refers to the editorial team that has been involved in the creation of this book. Ultimately, the real "we" of the book are the fellows who contributed to this book and others who participated in its creation in other ways. This "we" doesn't fit easily or completely into established boxes. We are people who embody and embrace many hyphenates in our descriptors or have taken career paths that look particularly twisty. We are the people who are willing to blaze new paths, who appreciate rough edges, and who want to learn surprising new things—about ourselves, others, and the world—even as we embark on projects that challenge what we mean by civic media. We want to be told that our work is disruptive and that it upsets some people but also be validated and affirmed in the heart, soul, and energy we pour into the world.

As editors, we carefully place ourselves within this book not to write about what we have learned but to learn and reflect alongside each other. For better and worse, we acknowledge the role we played in creating this fellowship. And we recognize that we share this platform with the fellows who gave it meaning and shape, making

Civic media is less of an object of study and more about the intentions of our practices and processes.

us all collaborators of change. The title, *We Are Civic Media*, is a testament to the collective nature of not only what is forthcoming in this text but of how civic media is led by us. We are actors, chefs, scholars, parents, content creators, artists, and members of communities that have strived yet struggled. We reclaim civic media to be about us. Civic media is less an object of study and more about the intentions of our practices and processes.

Our resistance and reclamation is not antagonistic, but in the nature of civic media, it is growing, healing, and uplifting. It is critical yet rooted in care. It relies and builds on the work of Cathy Cohen, Sasha Costanza-Chock, Eve Ewing, Eric Gordon, Henry Jenkins, Paul Mihailidis, and Ethan Zuckerman, among others, who have guided us intellectually to this space and worked to define, study, and grow civic media as we know it today. But how important is it to define what we mean by civic media when it is constantly changing? Does civic media actually need to be defined?

Cerianne Robertson, who worked with the Civic Media Fellowship while a doctoral candidate at the Annenberg School for Communication and Journalism, simply says to the question of "What is civic media?" that there is "no right answer." And by no means is that a lazy or unsophisticated answer but rather one that appreciates and acknowledges the diversity and dynamic nature of civic media work. Robertson claims, "There is a shared sense that there is no urgent need to define rigid boundaries around the field, and indeed that a strength of the field is its fluidity and creativity. Still, an emphasis on engaging a community or a public, combined with imagining how that community or public can change conditions for the better, seems to underscore almost all the fellows' work."

Centering historically marginalized approaches, people, and voices, we highlight cultural strategies, journeys, and domains of engagement. This collection explores lived practice and invites readers to consider how we build on and push beyond the existing boundaries of civic media.

What Do We Mean by "Civic"?

Civic media creators take a participatory approach to the "civic" or urgent social justice issues they face and the limiting, often oppressive, institutional, corporate, and organizational structures they navigate. They demonstrate new approaches to the creative process, socializing their work and engaging others in exploration and refinement of their ideas in powerful ways. These practices prioritize trust and connection. In the words of community organizer, media producer, archivist, curator, and educator Martha Diaz, "Civic media is about how we activate the community."

This unique relationship to the folks formerly known as the audience was an essential part of the initial creation of the fellowship, raising questions about the importance of participation and collaboration in this context and any associated expectations of prospective program participants. The MacArthur Foundation, for instance, signaled its view by titling their new program Participatory Civic Media. Deeper consideration of the people and practices that we saw as indicative, effective, and inspirational—and connected to the "meaningfully inefficient" dimensions of civic life[3]—underscored the fundamental importance of participatory approaches.

To be more precise, civic media creators are members of "civic" communities. They are also the mobilizers of communities and the innovators driving civic participation who raise the voices of the marginalized. In contrast to both traditional news media's performed objectivity (and resistance to making a call to action) and most folks' overwhelming sense of inefficacy vis-à-vis politics and public policy, civic media is explicitly about building trust, inspiring action, and empowering people.

Active participation through civic media suggests that people are engaged, while apathy or hostility might indicate that there are underlying issues requiring attention. Indeed, for creators and amplifiers alike, modest engagement is the essential first step to nurture a sense of individual and collective agency. Given the many complex and far-reaching challenges currently facing us at the local and global levels, the promise of increased participation in community and civic life is an invaluable resource.

The challenges practitioners face are often grand and deep-seated (or rooted in issues at that scale), which suggests a kinship with social movements. As such, this more inclusive approach along with an uncertainty mindset lends itself to longer-term approaches to deepening understanding, raising awareness, and changing how people participate. The ways in which people do the work—in community, with an eye to experimentation, dynamically—also have implications for experiencing joy, building power, and otherwise extending beyond tactical engagements.

Whereas mass media has historically been created and shared in ways that intentionally or functionally limit reuse, remix, and other forms of participation for purposes such as control and monetization, civic media makers see engagement—whether in the process or with its product—as a primary goal. They work with their intended communities in the creation of the text and by opening possibilities to engaging with it. This expands focus from the media object itself to what motivated, informed, created, accelerated, and otherwise gives meaning to it.

Indeed, while civic media practitioners incorporate a breadth of ideas, perspectives, and practices with particular audiences and gains in mind, they are

Civic media is about how we activate the community.

—MARTHA DIAZ

grounded in the uncertainty of outcomes. Although civic media work certainly has goals, its implications are often less about near-term results and more about the process of creation and the civic engagement, connection, and insight it fosters over time. Impact and experience are characterized by the opportunities established, the chances taken, and the collective learning and strengthening of communities.

While our experience and attention are substantially within the United States and these issues play out differently according to context, today's global interconnectedness and the local-global orientation of many populations (especially youth) mean that civic media participation may both be hyperlocal and have significant international ramifications. Through the civic media space, we see how transnational networks of media travel beyond political boundaries. Arshia Haq navigates the complexities of multiple identities and diaspora through Discostan, a collaborative decolonial project that reconfigures the nightclub and dance floor as radical spaces that rewrite the histories of South Asia, West Asia, and North Africa. Other fellows have used social media, filmmaking, and podcasts to amplify silenced voices, leveraging technology to counter warfare and injustices in the face of occupation. Although these movements are often developed at local and grassroots levels, civic media practices can help build and sustain transnational support networks, global movements, and international policy shifts.

Through breaking away from traditional media forms and approaches and engaging civic and community concerns and participation, practitioners create media with the intention to disrupt the status quo in novel ways. Through our collaborations, we have come to understand that civic media is practiced through seemingly more oblique approaches such as comedy, food, sex work, and quilting, alongside other more traditional yet innovative media of storytelling. Those creative, nonconventional, and disruptive vectors for change stand wonderfully (and powerfully) apart from the more traditional and goal-oriented ways in which civic engagement is typically advanced and conceptualized.

What Do We Mean by "Media"?

Drawing upon a wide range of cultural resources including food, history, gaming, dance, visual art, film, journalism, fashion, comedy, and much more, the creative changemakers in this book are better characterized by the novel ways in which they combine and reinvent practices and reconceive ideas to foster surprise, delight, and authentic engagement. They simply use the right platform for the moment, what our colleagues have termed "by any media necessary."[4]

We see civic media as those uses of technology—old and new—that promote justice, community, and civic action where the intention and agency of those creating the media and their identified beneficiaries take precedence. Whether it is to educate, engage, imagine, or activate, the goals of civic media depend on the intentions of the practitioner, not on a specific platform. Bucking media determinism and platform specificity, the contributors generally see media as the *mode*, not the substance, of their work. As filmmaker and virtual reality creator Paisley Smith notes, "Civic media relates to our history, our culture and community. . . . We feel called to make something and share with people because of our own experience or something we've heard of in past generations. We are moved to share for the greater good of our community. It's a quilt, or it's a book, or it's a film. It's this thing that has a life, that lives on, that shares a story."

From paintings to VR, from memes to events, civic media needs to meet people where they are to be relevant, useful, and engaging. These approaches also help to overcome some limitations of new and traditional media. Truly reaching people in terms of relevance, attention, and trust is a challenge for any communicator and arguably a core skill for civic media practitioners—in part due to a keen awareness of audience. They do not see their audience as "everyone" because they understand both that targeting everyone is effectively the same as targeting no one and that narrowly tailored communications actually often help to reach a broader audience.

Of course, in today's lightning-fast and interconnected world, the concept of working through "any media necessary" has become increasingly crucial, especially in the realm of civic media. This approach emphasizes the importance of sharing work (often analog) across multiple media platforms and adapting to their unique formats, norms, and audiences. In an age where information and communication technologies are constantly evolving, the ability to effectively use a diverse range of media platforms is vital for engaging in civic discourse and activism.

The contributors to this collection demonstrate remarkable proficiency in working through different media platforms, primarily because they craft compelling content and stories that they are eager to share. Their challenge is not in creating meaningful material but in identifying the most suitable medium to effectively disseminate their messages and engage their intended audiences. As the photographer, visual artist, and filmmaker SHAN Wallace (author of "Our Civic Media: Portraying My Community Through My Lens") says, "I wear a lot of hats and do a lot of things. I like to wake up and choose a medium that fits whatever idea that I have and want to manifest." Our contributors' adaptability and media savvy enable them to navigate various platforms deftly, ensuring their important narratives are heard and have a lasting impact.

Civic media is about intention rather than platform.

—TYREE BOYD-PATES

As such, members of this network invite us to think more boldly about civic media as stretching the boundaries of what we see as media. Latoya Peterson (see "United in Flow: Accessible Pleasure, Game Design, and How We Heal"), a storyteller and technologist, defines it succinctly: "Civic media is media for the public. One hundred percent full public." This sentiment is echoed and expanded upon by visual artist Susu Attar (see "Reflections on Process"), who reflects on using "media in any way, shape, or form. With a consciousness of community embedded into it." Tyree Boyd-Pates (author of "Museum Curation as Care: Civic Media, Black History, and Communicating Afrofuturist Imaginings"), a curator, writer, activist, and historian, perceives civic media as "multidisciplinary, interdisciplinary" and civic media creators as crossing boundaries while "retaining our cultural and community identities." As media maker Sue Ding (author of "Civic Media: A Space for Exploration") summarizes, "Civic media is about intention rather than platform."

So in putting all this together, the "we," "civic," and "media" in *We Are Civic Media* are much more process oriented, as much about the journey as the destination. We believe civic media allows us to dig deeper, imagine further, and become visible beyond these narrow goal-oriented actions. With an emphasis on community building and storytelling, civic media is about the validating of struggles, uplifting historically silenced narratives and voices, supporting those around you, and protecting those who are left behind. Civic media is not simply righting the wrongs but is about dismantling harmful histories while building foundations for communities to thrive in the present and for future generations.

So what can you expect from *We Are Civic Media*? We wrote this book to help field builders, stakeholders, educators, creative professionals, and community leaders who want to understand both the deeply personal human as well as the broader conceptual dimensions of civic media. Created through a process that aligns with our commitments to participation, this book is by people and about people. It takes a human-centered approach to civic media, one that foregrounds the lived experiences, struggles, concerns, solidarity, and aspirations of those who create and engage with civic media, whether they realize it or not. This is why each section of this book offers one of many possible paths through the contributors' lived experiences as civic media practitioners as they pursue their own journeys, projects, challenges, and joy. The stories shared deserve and need to be read as rich and complex both as their own pieces and alongside one another as a collection. These stories cannot be contained or put into limiting categories, so the structure we present here is an invitation to the reader to enter the world of our civic media and find their own paths and connections.

Movement and Community

This section of the book explores the themes of community, collective action, and personal identity. The authors delve into their experiences as individuals who have organized and participated in various movements, highlighting the joy and strength that can be found in coming together as a community. They also reflect on the challenges they faced in navigating their positions within their communities while emphasizing the importance of inclusivity and transparency in activism.

Journeys and Reflections

In this section, authors focus on their personal journeys and reflections. They share stories as individuals who have embarked on transformative life journeys. These journeys often involve struggles, discoveries, and self-reflection, leading to a deeper understanding of themselves and their commitments to their marginalized communities. This section connects the personal to community to global issues in centering the power of storytelling as a means of sustaining the struggle for justice.

Design and Care

The themes of design, care, and community are at the heart of this section. The authors share how they use design and creativity to foster healing and build communities. Whether it's through physical spaces, software, or artistic expression, the authors emphasize the importance of thoughtful design and genuine care in creating spaces and experiences that empower and uplift others while addressing the role of personal growth along the way.

Claiming and Reclaiming

The final section of the book revolves around the themes of reclaiming identity and challenging existing narratives. Here the authors explore how individuals and communities assert their identities and narratives in spaces that may not always recognize or value their voices. They critique mainstream media and stress the urgent need to decenter dominant narratives, offering alternative perspectives and commentary. In doing so, they dare to hope as they push back against oppressive norms and constraints.

If there is one thing we want you to take with you when you finish this book, it is this: Civic media making is not a destination. Civic media is about personal and networked journeys of artists, activists, and community leaders. Within these pages, you won't simply read about journeys; you'll journey alongside the storytellers, gaining profound insights into the transformative lessons and personal evolution experienced by these civic media practitioners. In sharing their accounts and stories, this collection serves as a rallying cry for cultural strategies, personal odysseys, and a myriad of engagement domains.

We Are Civic Media is a call to action and an invitation into this vibrant, emergent, and challenging space.

Notes

Epigraph: *Once Upon a Tech: A Comic Zine About the Future and Surviving the Digital Apocalypse*, June 15, 2021, https://issuu.com/uscannlab/docs/finalcomic_2. This zine was created by the Civic Media Fellowship at the USC Annenberg Innovation Lab and sponsored by the MacArthur Foundation.

1 Eric Gordon and Paul Mihailidis, eds., *Civic Media: Technology, Design, Practice* (MIT Press, 2022).

2 Carrie James, *Disconnected: Youth, New Media, and the Ethics Gap* (MIT Press, 2016).

3 Eric Gordon and Gabriel Mugar, *Meaningful Inefficiencies: Civic Design in an Age of Digital Expediency* (Oxford University Press, 2020).

4 Henry Jenkins, Sangita Shresthova, Liana Gamber-Thompson, Neta Kligler-Vilenchik, and Arely Zimmerman, "By Any Media Necessary: The New Youth Activism," in *By Any Media Necessary* (New York University Press, 2016).

Movement and Community

The Attempts to Hold It All

At the Intersection of Black Food Futurism and Civic Media

Nia Lee

Nia Lee (they/them/she/her) is an award-winning Black queer artist, chef, and organizer who intertwines traditional Black American archival food ways with innovative healing practices to craft unique and transformative food experiences. They are the originator of Black Food Futurism, and their groundbreaking work has garnered acclaim in prominent publications such as the *Los Angeles Times*, *The Cut*, *Thrillist*, and *Vogue* magazine and has been featured on Netflix's James Beard–nominated docuseries *High on the Hog*. In addition to her culinary artistry, Nia is the visionary behind Stormé Supper Club, a Los Angeles–based wine and dinner series that centers and celebrates queer Black women, femmes, and gender-expansive individuals.

There are parts of me that I do not talk about. Parts that sit at the bottom of a deep freezer in the back of a dusty, crowded two-car garage. Sitting beneath the blocks of frozen autumn squash soup and square boxes of store-bought pizza there's this thing wrapped in layers of saran wrap, crunchy silver aluminum foil, and brown twine. It's this ugly thing, freezer burned and hardened with time. It's frozen solid yet still has a beating heart that's alive with a deep slow pulse that murmurs rhythmically, each thud acting as the soundtrack for this little world of the deep freezer in the garage. The crunchy cold thud sounds like the little people partying in your pillow at night, a kind of thud that you can only hear when you are at your most quiet and still, when you listen beyond the hum of the deep freezer and sounds of life in the house. The heartbeat of this thing can only be heard when you are at your most quiet and still. But this thing is there and it always will be . . .

I'm an artist and food is my medium. Food is how I see the world. It's how I exist in the world. It's how I both contain and expand my world. It's what Octavia Butler would call a "positive obsession," and by some sweet black magic I've made a career out of it. It truly is a wonder that I get to do what I love every day.

In 2019 I started a queer dinner series centering Black and Brown queer women, femmes, and gender-expansive people. Named after the lesser-known lesbian icon and activist Stormé DeLarverie, this work seeks to honor her name and legacy while providing a space of expansiveness, connection, and joy for queer people today. I also understand this work to be an intentional art practice and participatory performance tied to my larger practice of what I call "Black Food Futurism," the intentional practice of merging Black food ways and art to imagine new ways of fostering community and creativity. Black and Brown queers taking up space in the name of exhalation, expression, and beauty is a powerful and audacious way to usher in new possibilities of being and thriving. I'm honored to be able to create a safe space for this way of Black queer unfolding through food and wine and to be someone who is adding to the dialogue around the ever-expansive Black food movement.

For the first time, people outside of my community are becoming interested in my food practice. They want to know more and to help. They want to photograph me and interview me. I'm talking to managers now, I have an agent who is helping me sell my books, and TV show producers email me about appearances. I am a "brand" now, and someone is always watching.

Over the years I've gotten somewhat good at explaining the many aspects of my work and my root philosophy when it comes to understanding my food practice and Black Food Futurism in general, but now people want to know about *me*. They ask, "So what made you choose food as your medium?" and "How did you get started in food?" and "Did you grow up in a food family?" For the first time they want to know not just about my work but about who I am as a person. They want to know my story.

I talk about my father and his passion for flavors and honoring the legacy of our Black food ways. I recount the annual pot of chitterlings that appears on the stove every New Year's Day. I talk about the visceral twang of vinegar, spices, and the distinct pungent smell of pig intestine wafting through our old New England house like a fog filled with memories. I talk about my mother and her commitment to exploring new ways to imagine Black food via imaginative Indigenous Black vegan food practices and how her father, my grandfather, used food to heal before Whole Foods was even a whisper. I say that I'm the perfect blend of my parents and that I hold the totality of Black food ways in my body.

I also talk about food being the sticky Velcro that holds humanity together. I talk about the after-church meal being my first understanding of food as a community builder and sacred connector. I recount a dining room filled with Bible-toting young people laughing over boldly seasoned homemade lasagna and orange juice from a frozen tube. The story is palpable, clear, and personable. This is the story that helped me get the Civic Media Fellowship, the fellowship that ultimately made it possible for me to do this work full-time. This is the story that makes sense. This is the story that goes down easy.

But this bio mythology is sprinkled with little lies—little withholdings perhaps is a better way to say it. These stories are true and do make up large parts of how I came to this work, but there are also giant holes in this narrative that don't fit nicely into my story.

"Re-memory," a term that Toni Morrison coined, speaks to the performative nature of memory. It's a core feature and thematic narrative in so much of Morrison's work. I see it as the act of massaging our memories like a baker kneads dough, pushing, pulling, and mixing to create strong strands of gluten. With memory, it's kneading to create strong strands of a self that one can use to make sense of things in the midst of so much senselessness. Re-memory is a powerful survival tactic for Black people living in these multiple layers and generations of forced and systemic ostracization and marginalization.

Food is the sticky velcro that holds humanity together.

When I think about the individual and communal traumas that Black people have faced for generations, it's a weight so heavy that it pushes me through to the other side of the earth. My brain can't even comprehend it. Naming it all would split my tongue in two. Naming it all would crack the entire world open and ooze yellow egg yolk magma into the universe. So I've learned, like my grandmother, and all of my grandmothers since the beginning of time, the art of re-memory. It's not ignoring hard truths but rather kneading our memories in a way that finds a lightness so we can keep living.

This line of thinking makes me wonder about the slow beating heart of the thing in the deep freezer. If I named it, would I also be able to survive? Would I have gotten this fellowship that sustained me for so long? I don't know, but I live in a world that makes me think that perhaps I wouldn't have.

The gluten strand of a memory that doesn't fit nicely into my story is that, quite literally, my food work isn't a choice. After decades of disordered eating, my brain has tuned itself to hyperfixate on food. I had a childhood where I felt I had no agency, power, consistency, safety, or voice, so I found something to fill that deeply human need for control: food.

I wonder how specific I should get. There's a part of me that wants to tell you about how the bathroom floor became my second bed and how the toilet became my coolest pillow. But as a ten-year-old I learned so many of my tactics from the glossy pages of *Teen Vogue*, *Seventeen*, and *CosmoGirl*, which were filled with harrowing stories of young women who came back from the brink of death from their disordered eating habits. Where I should have been reading these stories as cautionary tales, I took them as inspiration and learned the stealthy ways to hide the dangerous cycles of withholding, hyperfixation, and purging. These cycles became my best friends. These cycles became the only consistent thing in my life.

The women in my life also mirrored these habits in their own ways. Extreme diets, working out as punishment, and comments about other women's bodies taught me that the only thing to aspire to be was thin. And I was so thin. I look back at photos of myself as a child and teen and see my dark circles, yellowed teeth, pale skin, and little ribs starting to poke out from my early 2000s baby tees and wonder why no one else saw, and if they did, why nothing was done. I was clearly unwell, and somehow the women in my life said in big ways and small that there were always a few more pounds to lose.

I'm thirty-something now, and I'm the healthiest and heaviest I've ever been. Years of therapy have been a balm, but I still suffer from obsessive compulsive disorder, body dysmorphia, and an eating disorder that rears its head under high stress or whenever I have to spend time with family. Sometimes my brain is a tough place to be in. That's the truth of brain stuff and addictions: Parts of it will always be there. But through the art of re-memory and therapy I've been able to take my deep wounds and turn them into my gift. I come from a people that are masters at the art of transforming deep pain into art and progress, and I think that's what I'm doing with my food work today. My people were given the table scraps and created soul food. I was given a "neuro-spicy" brain and created Black Food Futurism.

Civic media, in its malleability, allows space for the complexities of art and action in a way that I'm not sure that other practices do. My work sits at so many intersections. It sits at the intersection of performance art, historical and archival narratives, Black food ways, Afrofuturist thinking, and community building, and civic media in practice and theory has been able to hold space for the vast Venn diagram of my work, all while giving me the safety and courage to be honest about all of the glutenous strands of memory and self that make up me and my story.

The world of civic media reminds us that the most poignant forms of civic engagement occur when we bring our full selves to the table and move from a place of curiosity and intention. It's bringing others into the fullness of our world to create a new one. I hope that you too will take stock of everything that's in the deep freezer and feel safe in knowing that the world can hold it all.

Self-portrait, courtesy of the author.

Being Together

The Revolutionary Love of a Poor People's Movement

Anu Yadav

Anu Yadav (she/her) is a critically acclaimed Indian-heritage actress, playwright, and cultural worker. She has performed at venues such as the John F. Kennedy Center for the Performing Arts, Shakespeare Theatre Company, and National Academy of Dramatic Arts in Beijing. She was the 2019–20 inaugural Creative Strategist Artist-in-Residence at the LA County Department of Mental Health, in partnership with the LA County Department of Arts and Culture. She is a 2023–25 Dramatists Guild Foundation Catalyst fellow and 2023 Race Forward Housing and Land Justice Artist fellow. Anu is a member of the Actors' Equity Association, Center for Performance and Civic Practice, Dramatists Guild, Network of Ensemble Theaters, We Cry Justice Artist Collective at the Kairos Center for Religions, Rights, and Social Justice, and the Poor People's Campaign: A National Call for Moral Revival. She is a graduate of Bryn Mawr College and holds an MFA in performance from the University of Maryland, College Park.

Love is an action
A place to sleep
Love is to rise up
Standing with me

Love is together
Righting the wrong
Knowing there's a place
You always belong

I had just come home from a theater rehearsal. I was standing on my front stoop, fumbling to find my keys, when I saw it: an eviction notice. It said the police were coming to remove me, my housemates, and all of our belongings in thirty days. No letterhead, just a plain white piece of paper with a business card taped to it. Over the next few weeks, my housemates and I scrambled to figure out what was happening. The owner of the house had defaulted on his mortgage and the house was now foreclosed on. The bank had sent a realtor threatening us with eviction. I spent countless hours trying to figure out our rights, get legal help, and talk with housemates to collectively agree on each step as the process and threats continued. It was an illegal eviction. They were counting on our fear and ignorance, but we wouldn't go easily.

Local housing organizer Miss Debra helped me jumpstart my research with a barrage of names and numbers of tenants rights resources. She was a genius. A wildly charismatic leader, she was protesting the displacement of her public housing community in southeast DC. I had joined her organizing six years before my own housing crisis, befriending her and other Black women fighting for their neighborhood. We were part of a multiracial movement to end poverty. But at the time I didn't think I was poor. I thought I was a middle-class ally. I had been interviewing Miss Debra and other residents while writing a play to highlight their organizing. I was a youth theater educator volunteering in the community. I didn't see myself as directly impacted. Reality, however, shattered that illusion into a thousand tiny pieces. In my crisis, love was an action—many actions—of being caught over and over again by the soft net of my community. It's taken me many years to realize that this movement to end poverty has always been mine too.

Author and poet Luis Rodriguez once told me, "When we're caught up in a crisis, creativity is a path out of it." For me, that creativity, forged with love and community, was a powerful path through. In my lowest moments, I created theater as a necessary, urgent means for survival. It is also the kind of creativity demanded of any poor person trying to survive in a society where poverty is the fourth leading cause of death. Throughout the process of navigating my eviction and other unfolding crises, I experienced the profound love of my community and movement and then poured that love back into theater and song. This movement reminded me there are so many of us, precariously, on the brink—140 million poor and low-wealth people in the United States who cannot afford a $400 emergency, with millions more just a paycheck away. I realized that my middle-class identity only separated me from other people in struggle and distorted the truth of my economic reality. I was poor. I could be again. And in our numbers there is power.

Break the lie of loneliness
Break it with love
There's a place for you
There's a place for us

A place for you
Here in my heart
Come right home
To the truth of my arms

To the truth of my arms

Friends and Residents

In 2002, I moved to DC, where I met Miss Debra. Her neighborhood was going to be torn down and redeveloped. Four hundred Black families, through no fault of their own, would be relocated and displaced from the Arthur Capper/Carrollsburg public housing projects, known as Cappers by its residents. It was near the Navy Yard—a stone's throw from Capitol Hill. She and others organized to fight for their housing rights. They called themselves Friends and Residents of Arthur Capper/Carrollsburg. The redevelopment was being funded by the HOPE VI federal grant program, touted on paper to be the first of its kind in the nation, promising one-to-one replacement of all low-income units. But organizers discovered they were redefining low-income as households making up to $60,000 per year. Households in the neighborhood made an average of $8,000 per year. That, along with other barriers, would allow developers to cherry-pick who returned. Residents knew developers just wanted them gone, but if the community organized, they could push to prioritize residents' needs and hopefully benefit. What developers saw only as a "blighted" community they could tear down for profit was actually a rich community—rich in love, pride, and lifelines of support. People had each other.

Miss Debra was one of Friends and Residents' leaders. Thin, wiry, and always on the move, Miss Debra had been part of the antiwar movement and the anti-apartheid movement and now brought her activism back home. Then there was Miss Rose, bighearted and energetic, always sweeping the porch of her sparklingly clean house. She had an ear to the ground and consistently whipped up the best snacks for meetings at her place. Miss Agnes was quiet, measured, stately—with a quick wit and the occasional raunchy joke. First in a walker and then an electric wheelchair, she didn't get out as much as the others but expertly wielded the phone. And Miss Mary was the local spiritual advisor who many leaned on for guidance and prayer. They were all movers and shakers in the neighborhood and made up the main advisory board of the organization. They meant business and welcomed people to help in the work. People like Todd, a young white organizer who had initially invited me to a community meeting. He had become a fixture in the neighborhood, winning trust with his passion, loyalty, and commitment.

Soon I was knocking on doors with them, helping with petitions and attending community meetings, and eventually I taught youth arts workshops. Every time I walked down L Street, children ages four to ten would come running up to me, eager, shining, and ready to play. They would pepper me with questions such as, "Can you do that thing you do with your chin?" (you can ask if we ever meet in person) or "You got a mustache. Why you don't cut it off?" (I'm a South Asian woman and sometimes you just gotta be you). Soon the youth trailblazed their own organizing effort to save the recreation center from being shut down before people moved. Young people ran around the neighborhood with homemade petitions, some drawn with crayon, amassing hundreds of signatures. The adults followed their lead and found out it was an illegal move on part of the District of Columbia Housing Authority. And the youth won. Love here ran deep even if the development completely disregarded that. But it would take more fights to demand things be different.

Out of many projects that we did as part of the organizing—running the gamut from community gardening to cleanups, poetry, and youth theater—I decided to interview residents and, with their permission, write a play. It would be a way to attract volunteers and start a public dialogue from residents' perspectives. The intensive listening process over the three years it took to create the play became a way to uplift people's experiences and build relationships.

It became a solo play, directed and codeveloped by Patrick Crowley, that I performed around DC and then nationally. Often Miss Debra, Miss Rose, or Miss Agnes would come and speak as well. It was an imperfect offering. I was a South Asian woman from the Midwest performing stories of Black people from DC. But the women I engaged as the advisory board were adamant the story needed to be told and felt a sense of ownership over the play too, even if through an outsider. They gave their blessing, and it drew the attention of filmmakers Ellie Walton and Sam Wild, who then produced a documentary on gentrification in DC called *Chocolate City*, for which they interviewed residents and shared their stories more widely. Art became a strategy to bring attention to the crisis of poverty and housing as well as to support the organizing campaign. At the time, I didn't fully understand what in my own life drew me to this community and this fight. That would come later.

At the end of that redevelopment process, Cappers experienced significant wins and losses. Miss Debra, Miss Rose, Miss Agnes, and many of the seniors came back. Most of the original residents did not. Housing prices continued to skyrocket, with more and more communities being devastated. Despite the wins, many more were losing their housing. Even Miss Debra and Miss Rose began organizing *again* when they returned to the newly built Cappers and discovered it would face yet another round of gentrification. It was clear we needed to not just fight locally but also build a movement.

Part of the organizing also involved connecting to a larger network of communities fighting across different issues, like the right to water in Detroit or the fight against mountaintop removal in West Virginia. We connected with these groups through the Poverty Initiative in New York (now the Kairos Center for Religions, Rights, and Social Justice). The members of these groups led human rights tours and exchanges, convening from a diverse range of poor and working class communities so they could remember they were not alone in their struggle. Beyond that, they could learn and strategize together. We could build a movement. Cappers even became a destination on a national human rights bus tour that a multiracial group of leaders of low-income constituents were taking to document and submit human rights violations to the United Nations. This became another way to break isolation, connecting people who didn't even know each other existed to build power together.

Emerging from decades of organizing, in 2018 this expanding network joined with another organization, Repairers of the Breach, to launch the Poor People's Campaign: A National Call for Moral Revival, a social movement in more than forty states led by the poor across many lines of difference. It aims to take up the mantle of Dr. Martin Luther King Jr.'s original 1968 Poor People's Campaign, which brought together a multiracial "army of the poor" to end the "triplets of evil": systemic racism, systemic poverty, and the war economy. The new campaign took on these same goals, adding a fourth—ecological devastation. By backing the leadership of poor people across color lines, we could be what King called a "new and unsettling force in our complacent national life" in his 1967 speech "Nonviolence and Social Change"—a force that could ignite the political will to radically transform society.

Out of the mud
The lotus blooms
Hearts wide open
With the truth

Seeking justice
Seeking peace
Linking arms
We're gonna get free

Creativity in Crisis

People would call Miss Mary from across the country for prayer. Known as the Cappers neighborhood prophet, she said what was happening there was just the beginning of a larger crisis that would impact more people in the city. Even people making $30,000 to $60,000 a year or more were just a paycheck away from being homeless. Organizing at Cappers was a way to staunch the flow of injustice that was bound to spread. It followed a legacy of housing segregation and displacement of Black and poor communities in many cities. The federal grant program HOPE VI had been conducting these demolitions and displacements since the Clinton presidency. We were in her living room, the air conditioner rattling, in between her phone meetings for prayer. I remember nodding. Miss Mary was right. When I got the eviction notice on my door years later, I remembered her words. It was the first of many cracks in my middle-class identity.

When I was growing up, we always had food on the table, but we still struggled. After my dad died, my mom juggled night shifts at Burger King and community college while raising me and my younger brother. It wasn't easy, but it also wasn't named as the poverty it was. Stigma silenced us and limited our understanding of our situation. It also cut off connection to others in crisis. Slowly but surely, I began to put the pieces together. Every now and then my mom would share another bit of information, "If it wasn't for your dad's Social Security, I don't know what we would have done" or "I thought about seeking refuge in a church." That stopped me in my tracks. We are Hindu. It was telling.

As I was dealing with the illegal eviction, the mothers at Cappers stepped in to advise. We had stayed connected, built real relationships, and they knew what to do. Miss Debra suggested hitting up Georgetown Law School's free legal clinic. She had a personal contact there. She checked in with me periodically as I navigated the situation. My housemates and I fought it with pro bono legal help and got paid out to move, but we scrambled to find affordable housing as rents continued to soar.

Miss Debra handed me a slip of paper with the numbers for Medicaid, food stamps . . . and public housing. For that last one I could get on a list seven years long, but there were other more immediate resources I could be eligible for. That's when it hit me: The people I thought I was the ally to were helping me. We were helping each other. For so many years I was committed to supporting other people's stories of struggle. But this time I was facing my own. And it wouldn't be the last time.

Years later when I lost my housing, income, and healthcare in one single month, I realized that without a fixed address, I was part of the uncounted homeless. Miss Agnes, among many others, offered me a place to stay. I still remember one day getting off at the wrong metro stop three different times. I had forgotten where home was that night. Another friend gave me her place while she was experiencing her own health nightmare of breast cancer and a double mastectomy. I remember looking at my bulging keychain, marveling at how many house keys I had. As much as I was terrified, I was also moved and profoundly humbled by the generosity and love surrounding me. A community was catching me where larger society had failed us all.

I wrote and performed a play, not despite my crisis but because of it. The play, *Meena's Dream*, is about a South Asian girl with a big imagination who alternates between fantasy and reality to cope with her mother's failing health. One day she comes home and reads a sign on her front door: Eviction Notice. After lightly explaining it away as a fun car adventure, her mother hides out in the bathroom. This moment underscores the mounting tensions in her life, of unpaid bills, food insecurity, and chronic health issues—poverty. In her lowest moment, she prays to a god she doesn't believe in.

A theater company agreed to produce the play. I orchestrated a community engagement strategy to bring in audiences. The play was sold out. Sparked by impressive publicity, the line outside sometimes formed two hours before the show. One area theater leader remarked she had never seen such diverse audiences across age, class, race, or ethnicity in her forty years of theatergoing. People were hungry for stories of hope that reflected back the truths they felt in their own lives. The play lifted up the contradictions of a for-profit healthcare system, and through the eyes of a child we could all remember our own imagination and desire for our fundamental right to health.

But the stress of everything was still wearing at me. I remember asking myself, "Is this the lowest point? What about this? Is *this* the lowest point?" Don't they always say when someone reaches their lowest point, things have to get better? I had to force myself to ask a different question, "OK, now what?" over and over and over again. One day I decided to reach out to places where I had performed in the past and soon secured one well-paying gig to perform the play. Creativity, with love and community, was starting to feel like a real way through, one step at a time. My art had begun as documentary style, listening to other people in their hardest struggles, and then evolved to facing my own truth. But I still carried shame about my own housing struggles. It has only been in the past few years that I publicly testified for the first time. In 2017 the Poor People's Campaign held a mass meeting at McCarty Memorial Christian Church in Los Angeles. I shared my story alongside

Anu Yadav shares her personal testimony at a Poor People's Campaign event, September 19, 2017, McCarty Memorial Christian Church, Los Angeles. Image courtesy of Fusion Films.

other directly impacted leaders. As I stood at the pulpit, something in me changed at a cellular level. The boom of my voice bounced off the cathedral walls to an audience of hundreds and an online audience of tens of thousands. It scared me. *The power of my voice scared me.* I reeled back from the microphone, took a breath, and kept going.

I trembled for thirty minutes afterward. Luis Rodriguez happened to be in the audience along with his wife, Trini Rodriguez, a healer, artist, and leader in her own right. We had become friends by this point. Luis found me in the alcove and said, "You are a beautiful person. Can I hug you?" I nodded. His warm embrace eased my shaking for a moment.

Later I sat next to Luis and Trini. I whispered to Trini, "I've never done that before." She nodded and gently touched my head with hers. "It changes you," she said.

She was right. I was poor and I did not need to feel ashamed. We were all part of the 140 million poor, and we were taking action together.

We are not broken
We are not too much
We are powerful
We are enough

We are enough

We Belong Together

Peppered throughout this essay are lyrics from a song I wrote called "We Belong Together." It emerged from collective study with artists across the country coordinated by the Kairos Center on love. We read *We Cry Justice: Reading the Bible with the Poor People's Campaign*, essays by movement leaders on poor people's quest for healing, justice, and freedom. While I identify as a theater artist, I never considered myself a songwriter. But I was inspired and reminded that creativity belongs to us all. We were studying revolutionary love.

In Hinduism "bhakti" refers to the purest form of devotion and surrender to God, with the understanding that God dwells within us all and therefore we, all of life, and the earth, are godly. It is similar to "agape," a Greek word in the New Testament that Dr. King uplifted as "the love of God operating in the human heart." We as a society must rise to embody agape and bhakti: a creative, redemptive, unconditional, and unsentimental kind of love. It is the only kind of love that will save us. To organize society around this love is to reorganize society from the bottom up until there is abundance and dignity for us all.

Being part of this movement, understanding my own poverty, and connecting across differences have allowed me to more deeply understand and feel glimpses of this love. I felt it in Cappers, when Miss Debra handed me the number for Medicaid, when Miss Agnes offered me a place to stay. I also felt it in Luis's hug after my testimony and Trini's gentle touch to my forehead. I feel it when I facilitate storytelling workshops in communities across the country, like with Chaplains on the Harbor, an organizing group composed of members from Aberdeen, Washington state's poor, mostly white, rural community. I felt like I was with family. Through this movement, I have felt the sweetness of connection and become more keenly aware of how we have been systematically isolated from each other. *Being together to build a movement is a practice in revolutionary love.* And we must engage in this practice daily, truly understanding who is poor today and why. We who are poor, we who are on the brink, and we who wanna throw down. And together, we can be that unstoppable, transforming force to make real that irresistible, seemingly impossible, blazingly bright future we all deserve.

We belong, we belong
We belong, we belong
We belong together

We belong, we belong
We belong, we belong
We belong together

Eavesdropping as Solidarity Tactic

Tanzila Ahmed

Tanzila "Taz" Ahmed (she/her) is a political activist, storyteller, and artist based in Los Angeles. She creates at the intersection of counternarratives and culture-shifting as a South Asian Muslim second-generation immigrant American woman. Taz has turned out over 500,000 Asian American voters, recorded five years of the award-winning *#GoodMuslimBadMuslim* podcast and makes #MuslimVDay cards annually. Her essays have been published in the anthologies *New Moons*, *Pretty Bitches*, *Good Girls Marry Doctors*, and *Love InshAllah*, and her poetry has been commissioned by the Center for Cultural Power, PolicyLink, KPCC's Unheard LA, and more. In July 2023, her first solo visual art show, *Aunties with Deadly Stare*, was exhibited at LA Artcore, and her art has been shown at the Eiteljorg Museum and the Smithsonian APA Center. A protest sign she designed is in the Smithsonian Museum of American History. Her latest poetry collection, *Grasping at This Planet Just to Believe*, was published April 2024 with Writ Large Projects.

The venue was jam-packed with Los Angeles's brightest and boldest Browns at the sold-out show. These weren't the typical South Asian doctors and engineers at your parents' parties. These were the troublemakers: the artists, the do-gooders, and the ones likely pushed to the margins by both mainstream society and the insular Brown community. We were the lone Desi rebels, until an event like this—the Swet Shop Boys concert on election night, 2016—brings us all together. As I scanned the dimly lit crowd, I could see the faces of activists I had marched with side by side in protests and musicians I had sung along to as they belted out about the revolution. These weren't just colleagues or friends—these were *my* people.

In the back lobby, that night's election coverage was projected wide and in full color on the wall. A handful of people were sitting around intently staring at the results coming in. It was still early—the polls in Los Angeles had just closed, but the results for the East Coast were coming in, and not for the candidate we wanted. The candidate who was winning had run on Islamophobic rhetoric. It seemed like every other week he was spewing some other anti-Muslim comment, which led to an escalation of hate incidences against anyone that "looked" Muslim.

I should know—every month I'd go through the news of the past month and talk about every major anti-Muslim incident on our podcast *#GoodMuslimBadMuslim*. When comedian Zahra Noorbakhsh and I started the podcast in January 2015, we didn't set out to create a political podcast; we were simply two Muslim women on the margins of mainstream White society and the Muslim community who had something to say. And we thought we were funny. In addition to talking about the latest hot topics, we had segments like "Awkward-Ask-a-Muslim," where we discussed awkward microaggressions that happened to us; we declared fatwas; we gave out "Good Muslim Awards"; and we reported on the latest "Creeping Sharia," the subtle ways Islam was seeping into the mainstream.

As our podcast entered 2016, it seemed more and more of our conversations revolved around either Islamophobic presidential campaign rhetoric or an anti-Muslim incident that was fueled by frenzied, stereotyped, media hysteria. People kept asking for the podcast to be released with more frequency, but reporting on hate against our people took an emotional toll and once a month was all I could handle.

As I waited in the audience for the Swet Shop Boys to come on stage, people kept asking me about the outcome of the election. I had worked in electoral politics for two decades, and I suppose punditry was something I was supposed to know. Despite having spent the past two years reporting on all the hate against Muslims, I was feeling optimistic. The results that were coming in for the Right were to be expected—they were coming in from red states. I knew once the results moved west, that the blue states would turn blue. The band was waiting until the election results were secured before they officially came out to perform. I told people that Islamophobia was an extremist campaign tactic and the average American wouldn't fall for it. We had seen hate, but we had also seen an uprising of Muslim and South Asian activists working on the front lines to counter the Islamophobia and create powerful narrative change. I should know—I had spent two years talking about it.

It was late when Riz and Heems of the Swet Shop Boys finally took the stage. Gone was their typical braggadocious swagger. Heems walked around morose, and Riz had a fire in his eyes. The swing states that were supposed to turn blue turned red, and everyone in the entire space was deflated.

Then the room erupted, singing along defiantly: "TSA always wanna burst my bubble" and "Inshallah, mashallah, hopefully no martial law," a chorus that would later be chanted as a protest anthem at airports during the Muslim ban shutdowns. The room was electric and grew progressively energized with each song. Even if we lost the election, we hadn't lost the war. We would not let our Brown skin be used as a tool of dehumanization. We would continue to be in community and protect each other. We would not be silenced.

As the show ended, Riz paused before looking at the audience intently and saying, "Don't get sad, don't get angry, get active and fight. This isn't the end. Get out there and fight."

I'll never forget what rapper Humble the Poet said as we exited the show. I commented how it was nice that we had a safe space like this concert to process the elections. He said, "There is no such thing as a safe space—we are people of the revolution."

That's right—every space we were in was a center point of revolution. But maybe it could be both safe *and* revolutionary.

ooo

The next morning, I woke up to a stream of apologetic texts and DMs saying "I'm sorry" from friends and strangers alike. Overnight, the results had come in, and the candidate whose campaign relied on hating people like me had won. I felt defeated.

I had spent the past two years covering Muslim America and had a genuine belief in the power of counternarrative storytelling to shift hearts and minds. I also felt scared, having fully internalized the threats against Muslims. At the time, the fear was very real. So many people had died already. Would we be sent to camps? Would the hate crimes against our community escalate? How will I protect myself and protect my family against these threats? How would I now survive?

The "I'm sorry" and "what should we do?" texts filled me with rage. The apology felt empty, like they had waited until it was too late to do anything. It moved the accountability off of them and onto me—like, "I'm sorry that YOU are going to have to deal with a much harder life now." Through my solidarity activism work, I felt strongly that our struggles were tied up with each other. We all needed to be united. The "sorry" texts felt like disavowal, a betrayal—betrayed by people who waited until the after election to ask what they should do when we had had a whole election season of hateful anti-Black and -Brown rhetoric, which wasn't enough of a motivation for these peers of mine to take action.

I had done my part to humanize myself, to do the song and dance to make Brown people like me relatable. Now it was their responsibility to see and protect that humanity.

ooo

The *#GoodMuslimBadMuslim* podcast started off as a Twitter joke making fun of podcasts. These were the days of Buzzfeed listicles and clickbait titles to garner traffic that would maximize virality of content. Back in those days the only people who had podcasts were overly earnest host types—each episode featuring a celebrity personality trying to gain audience through escalation of sensationalism. For all of 2014, Zahra and I would tweet at each other satire of what we thought a podcast about Muslims would include. "Hijabi-Doing-Something-First" was constantly in the news as well as some twisted version of Muslims experiencing a "normal" life. All the content was framed for the White gaze—but spaces for Muslims telling Muslim stories for Muslims were few and far between.

It was confusing to be a Muslim in America and see how Muslims were being awkwardly covered by the mainstream media—we were both powerful terrorist threats and disempowered exotics—and the contradictory roles we were placed in by the mainstream narrative were just silly. Silly with dire consequences. Our satiric tweets back and forth made fun of this awkward and problematic intersection—we used the hashtag #GoodMuslimBadMuslim after Mahmood Mamdani's book, which talked about this problematic intersection of being seen as both the good Muslim and the bad Muslim.

We tweeted about Burka bikinis and Muslim Christmas and halal bacon. Our followers asked us where they could find the podcast—they said that they had searched and it wasn't there. We had to tweet back at them that it was a joke making fun of the sensationalism of podcasts and the contradictions of Muslims in the mainstream media. It took us a year of running this gag before we wondered if we should move forward with making it a reality.

We launched our podcast the month after the first season of *Serial* had come to an end. There had been a boom in the podcasting market, and people were hungry for the next thing to listen to. We didn't have the fancy podcasting tools that exist today. I recorded on a borrowed $99 Blu Mic, and we edited on Garage Band—the free audio editing tool on a MacBook. To keep it simple we recorded in a straight shot, with minimal editing. We recorded at my dining room table at my apartment in Koreatown and knocked on the downstairs neighbor's door to get him to stop playing the guitar.

Our strategy was simple: Have an engaging conversation that just happened to be funny. Three five-minute-long hot topics, four quick pithy topics, keep it to thirty minutes. We would talk about being Muslim, but we wouldn't be spiritual or political—we would talk about being Muslim Brown women and finding our complex selves and all the contradictions we held. Our conversations were funny and brought out the best of each other—and we simply wanted to share that.

We quickly became newsworthy. The sound bite that we were bacon-eating, sex-having Muslim women was just too tantalizing for the mainstream media at a time when only a certain kind of good Muslim narrative was being touted. Of course, Zahra's acid reflux kept her from eating bacon, and I was going through a dating drought, so technically, we were *not* bacon-eating, sex-having Muslims. But the media didn't care. We were shiny and brand new. We were breaking boundaries just by being ourselves and talking about stories we wanted to talk about. Zahra was a Persian Shia comedian married to a White guy, and I was a South Asian Sunni political strategist, single and looking. She watched horror movies and listened to techno music, and I watched rom-coms and listened to punk. Our perspectives on life were different enough that our podcast conversations were discoveries, and sometimes even in opposition.

That first year, *Mother Jones* called us "part *Wayne's World*, part *Chicken Soup for the Teenage Soul*"; NPR called us "a podcast that disrupts the narrative"; and Oprah's *O* magazine said, "Everyone should listen to this podcast." We were getting fan mail from Ottawa, Sydney, Botswana, London, Pakistan, and France. We thought we recorded our podcast for people like ourselves, but it turned out the specificity in our storytelling had a wide appeal. We were making people laugh worldwide.

Our perspectives on life were different enough that our podcast conversations were discoveries, and sometimes even in opposition.

ooo

"Can you be sure to define your terms? I don't understand all the Muslim words you use and it makes it difficult for me to follow." I read the tweet aloud to Zahra. We were meeting a couple of months after our podcast had started. "I think we only said 'Inshallah' and 'Ramadan.' How are we supposed to define those terms?"

"Well, we need to define terms so all kinds of people can understand us. I have to define terms for my one-woman show all the time," Zahra responded. She was in the middle of producing her one-woman show in San Francisco, to a mostly liberal White audience in a black box room.

"But do we *want* this show to be for all kinds of people?" I replied. "I'm not interested in making a podcast for the White gaze. I'm interested in making a podcast for the one lonely Brown kid in the middle of Nebraska so she feels less lonely. If other people listen, that's fine. But it's not for the White gaze. Besides, it stilts the conversation to have to define words. If they don't understand a term, they can Google it."

Thus began the first of many behind-the-scenes heated debates we had over the course of our podcast. My personal audience of readers and listeners from my blogs and columns had always been South Asian or Asian. In fact, I started writing stories for and about my community of South Asian Americans after I started getting them out to vote—I realized telling stories about South Asian Americans was deeply intertwined with getting them to feel politically empowered enough to get civically engaged. A stand-up comedian in the Bay Area, Zahra had perfected her comedy to be heard by the liberal Whites who would frequent comedy clubs. Her stories were often the first time White people interacted with a funny Muslim woman. And the audience she brought to the podcast were these people.

To create for the White gaze or the Brown gaze?

Now it seems like a silly debate—the culture has shifted significantly in the past decade, and the idea of "recentering the narrative" is no longer a hot topic. There are many podcasters out there who tell their own perspective without considering the White gaze as their primary filter. By the late 2010s, telling specific stories about BIPOC communities became on trend in all storytelling forms. In podcasts, movies, books, and TV shows, everyone was trying to tell these BIPOC stories—sometimes poorly, but they were trying. But in 2015, it felt like a weighty topic—how would we build an audience if we didn't hold the hand of the majority audience to help them along?

By the end of that day, we decided we wouldn't define ourselves on the podcast. It was a difficult conversation that we would come back to time and time again. We would ask questions authentically—we wouldn't take on a dumb-blonde persona in an effort to elicit more questions of each other. We would rather just be ourselves. There were enough differences between our cultures and spiritual practices where we could actually ask for definitions from each other. But if it was basic general Muslim knowledge, people could just Google it.

Our conversations on the podcast got easier after that. We told our listeners that if they didn't understand something, they could Google the term and that it wasn't our responsibility to teach. We were here to level up and talk. We might have lost a few listeners that episode, but those weren't the listeners we wanted anyway. Our podcast didn't exist to humanize Muslims for the Others—we knew we were human, and we expected our audience to treat us accordingly without us dumbing it down for them.

ooo

It was five days after the election, and I had committed to give the keynote at a diversity conference at Texas State University long before, when I thought the election results would be different. As I stood at the podium for my keynote talk, I locked eyes with the cop standing at the back leaning against the wall. It was the first time I'd ever had a policeman in the room with me for a presentation. He had tightly cropped blond hair, a gun strapped to his waist, and a chunky bulletproof vest on. His arms were folded across his chest as he looked at me without seeing me. I shouldn't have been surprised—I had asked for him after all.

Specifically, I had asked about the security protocol for the conference. It's not something I had ever asked for before, but with the escalation of attacks against Muslims and the escalation of visibility our podcast had received, it was something I was concerned about. In the week leading up to the conference, an anonymous group calling themselves "Texas State Vigilantes" had distributed flyers on campus, with a picture of five men wearing camouflage and holding guns in front of an American flag. Next to them was the text "Now that our man TRUMP is elected and republicans own both the senate and the house—time to organize tar & feather VIGILANTE SQUADS and go arrest & torture those deviant university leaders spouting off all this Diversity Garbage." The flyers were posted with tape in the campus bathrooms.

In August 2016, just two months before my keynote, the "campus carry" legislation had passed in Texas. Now anyone could walk on campus with a concealed gun, legally. In response to this new legislation, that year the organization Cocks Not Glocks was running a Texas-wide campus campaign encouraging students to bring dildos to campus—in Texas it is illegal to own more than six "obscene devices," whereas there is no limit to the amount of guns one can own. Gun laws in California are drastically different (thank you, Black Panther Party!), and being afraid of getting shot while speaking was a risk that I didn't know I had to fear. After the elections and the hate crimes, I knew I had to be more proactive about my self-defense if I wanted to continue to be outspoken and speak in different states.

I was introduced to the policeman in the green room earlier—he assured me of my safety and the staff assured me about their extra security protocols. He was about my age and seemed nice enough. But I was staunchly anti-cop—my activism work taught me that the government was constantly surveilling my community and was heavily inclined to criminalize us.

There's a point in my keynote presentation where I talk about our 2014 AAPI Artists Delegation to Ferguson one hundred days after the police shooting of Mike Brown. I use it as an example to talk about using radical art and building interracial/intermovement solidarity. I stammered as I locked eyes with the cop at this point of the presentation. That night in Ferguson, we'd stood in front of the Ferguson Police Department and listened to comedians Jenny Yang and D'Lo tell corny cop jokes. In retelling the story, I talked about how much I loved that we used humor as a tool for social justice. I kept looking at the cop to see if he was listening.

After my keynote, students came up to me and said I was inspiring, called themselves radical changemakers, and felt energized to take action. They told me how they had a solidarity protest earlier that week and how Trump kids were trying to pick fights with them. When they asked how people could stand in solidarity with Muslims on campus, I stumbled, unsure of what could possibly be empowering at a place that felt like such a front line. Another hijabi student jumped in to rescue me from the conversation and offered herself up, saying that if anyone had any questions about Islam, they could ask her. She was confident that the problem lay just in the approach to the conversation. On the other hand, I felt no confidence.

That night, back at my hotel room, all I could reflect on was why the policeman got the bulletproof vest and not myself or these radical change-making youths.

ooo

There were two camps of anti-Islamophobia work that came out in that late-2010s era of activism: The first one was Muslims-Are-Just-Like-Us and on the other side was We-Can't-Be-Boxed-In. Obviously, with the title of *#GoodMuslimBadMuslim*, our podcast was in the latter camp. Immediately after the elections it became clear that the anti-Muslim bias was more mainstream than we thought.

On one side of the spectrum, the eager Muslims-Are-Just-Like-Us Muslims optimistically felt that all that was needed was to show White Americans that Muslims were Normal People. Suddenly, there were Muslims on the sides of the street holding signs that said "Hug a Muslim" to try and encourage empathy. Videos were being produced like "The Secret Life of Muslims" and "Meet a Muslim," with a parade of diverse Muslims having everyday interests, or "Dear Muslim Child," which shared the narrative of parenting a Muslim child. The token hijabi woman was being awkwardly written into everyday television sitcoms. Hasan Minhaj got a comedy special on Netflix, and Ramy Youssef started making his series for Hulu. A hijabi model in a full burkini was featured in the swimsuit edition of *Sports Illustrated*, and a Shepard Fairey illustration of a woman's face in an American flag hijab was put on a poster and carried by thousands at the Women's March. A campaign was started to invite a Muslim friend to your non-Muslim parents' Thanksgiving dinner and to have a difficult conversation with them. Documentarians were scrambling to find Muslim subjects to put on camera. Suddenly White people were trying so hard to humanize Muslims for the rest of America and Muslims were trying to humanize ourselves just to survive.

On the We-Can't-Be-Boxed-In side, Muslims were organizing spaces for ourselves and being disruptors. All kinds of books were being published in 2017 for and by Muslim writers (*Halal If You Can Hear Me*, *How to Be a Muslim*, *Muslim Cool*, *Letters to a Young Muslim*, *Home Fire*, *American Islamophobia*). Encrypted chat groups popped up, circulating actions and petitions. When people started descending on airports after the Muslim ban executive order was signed, it was organized through these chats. A campaign I ran featured Asian American poets reading solidarity poems on the steps of the Supreme Court during the Muslim ban hearings. I trained young Muslim activists at the first national Muslim Voter Convening in Atlanta, teaching them to turn out their community to vote and how to find Muslims in the voter database. We organized Muslim women to get self-defense training and started walking around with switchblades. We taught each other how to scrub personal data from the internet so we wouldn't be doxxed and took extra digital security measures so we wouldn't be surveilled. When a hate crime happened, we held vigils where we prayed together, read poems out loud to each other, and cried as a community.

And then there were the safety pins. Those stupid safety pins.

Someone somewhere decided that wearing a safety pin would become a secret allyship calling card—that by wearing a safety pin they would signal to Muslims that they would be their ally on a train, plane, or public space. The safety pins took on a life of their own, as it allowed so-called allies the ability to feel like they did something without ever having done anything. People were selling them on Etsy, beaded and different colored—and our podcast was getting so many emails from people saying they were sorry this was happening to us and that they were wearing a safety pin in solidarity. I was carrying a knife in my purse—I didn't need their safety pins to keep me safe.

When we finally released the next episode of our podcast after Election Day, titled "Pins and Polls," our conversation was deeply defeated. Our listeners were waiting to hear what actions to take next, but instead, we just cried and expressed our sadness. We stumbled through our anger at people who didn't vote and people who were so falsely confident in the Left's win that they didn't bother talking to the right-leaning moderates in their community. It wasn't a teachable moment for the White gaze; it was a deep commiseration and sharing of the feelings of fear we were feeling.

I uploaded two items to our online store that month. If people really felt like our podcast was important for this difficult time, they could make a donation to keep it running. And if they felt really strongly about safety pins and that it was about the symbolism of it all, they could purchase the *#GoodMuslimBadMuslim* limited edition safety pin for $2,020. The message on the website said, "Your purchase will help cover the cost of our podcast, as well as the registration cost of the forthcoming Muslim Registry."

Immediately, we got irritated emails from our non-Muslim listeners:

"I completely understand the backlash against the safety pin, because I think a lot of white folks will put one on their jacket and forget about it. . . . I want to earn the right to wear it with my actions and direct support."

"One of you asked, where were we in 2002 when the Muslim registry first started, and my shitty but honest answer is, not fully engaged. While I can't afford a $2,020 safety pin, I will continue to wear the one I dug out of my sewing box. But not to be 'liberal chic,' because while it is the absolute very least I can do, it will certainly not be all that I do."

"It feels insulting for you to sell a pin for $2,000 on your website because I feel like you're assuming the white women who would wear pins are rich white women and you're falling into the same stereotyping trap that those who marginalize tend to do."

"I just want to say that for us 'liberal white folks' the safety pin was a way in our frustration of showing that we aren't voters for the fascist dictator and that we stand for and with the civil rights of all and we will not be silent."

No one ever did buy our safety pin, but it got the satirical point across. That year, we asked our listeners to put their money where their mouths were and we were finally able to raise enough funds to cover our production costs and kept raising money till the end of our show. We were an independent and self-produced podcast, and every dollar mattered. It showed us that people actually believed that our words mattered.

We also started getting other kinds of emails and DMs too. I thought that because we had so explicitly centered our conversations on our lived experiences as Muslim thirty-something women, that was our audience. But we had all kinds of people listening to our show—and a surprisingly large amount of non-Muslim middle America. We never changed our podcast to speak to their gaze; they just happened to find and listen in to our show. They never expected our narrative to change because they joined to listen and they simply listened.

One person mentioned how sometimes it was difficult for them to listen to our show because they would have to do research to understand what we meant, but they enjoyed it. Another said it felt like they were listening in on a conversation between their two older sisters and just had to figure out what we were talking about through context clues.

"I'm a white woman that lives in a rural area in Wisconsin right outside the liberal bubble of Madison. I know I have built in assumptions about the world and listening to your podcast roots those out for me. Very refreshing and I'm learning so much."

"For what it's worth: Thanks for your podcast and being out there. As a middle aged white guy I appreciate hearing your voice and begin to understand in a small way life in America for other people."

As people of color, we are told to humanize ourselves by making ourselves easier to understand for mainstream White people, that we have to simplify ourselves to make ourselves more palatable, and that we should "dumb down" our perspective so we can be understood by the masses. We BIPOC folks had been so dehumanized and marginalized by mainstream society that we had to be extra simple to make ourselves human. But what I learned from the response our podcast received was that we didn't actually need to do that. If we expect our audience to level up, they will level up. By recentering the gaze on our specific lives, other people were able to relate—because these experiences are universal. There is a universality in sharing specific stories and being able to empathize with each other through truly listening to each other's narratives.

Our podcast allowed people to eavesdrop into inner-community conversations that were previously held behind closed doors. And by allowing this space for intentional listening—and expecting people to listen without responding as the podcast format is set up to do—we were finally able to speak our mind uninterrupted and create a platform for a different kind of solidarity building: eavesdropping.

ooo

In my Countering Islamophobia workshop I developed (and still train on) for a South Asian youth activist camp in 2011, I walk participants through various solidarity tactics to dismantle Islamophobia. The training's curriculum took a fifty-fifty approach—you had to push back through political change (voting, advocacy, civic engagement) and also push back through cultural change (counternarrative, pop culture, social shifts). The two went hand in hand, and change couldn't happen without both.

Though there had been a violent racial backlash after the 9/11 attack in 2001, it was silly to think that the sentiments fueling anti-Muslim hate a decade later were still considered "backlash." The Islamophobia had become systematized and turned into a well-funded multimillion-dollar industry. Between 2017 and 2019, thirty-five organizations funneled $105 million into anti-Muslim causes, according to a report from the Center for American Progress. Anti-Muslim hate wasn't simply a personal opinion that could change hearts and minds over coffee; there was a system in place to make hating Muslims possible. Countering Islamophobia had to be just as strategic and take down the whole system of hate.

In these workshops, participants brainstorm various tactics—from creating narrative-driven content to making disruptive art: vigils, protests, op-eds in the local press, and billboards; intimate conversations and widely broadcasted speeches; registering people to vote and talking to your elected officials; making posters and chalking sidewalks. Everything was a potential tactic.

Being a Muslim activist and content maker, with a lifetime of registering Muslims to vote and making art to politically empower Muslim Americans, I never would have imagined that the best tactic to build empathy would be to create a space for eavesdropping on real conversations. It really was just as simple as that.

ooo

The thing no one tells you about growing old is how you can literally measure time by cultural shifts. I have now been working as a political activist for twenty-five years, and it has been five years since the end of our podcast's five-year run. Making podcasts is very "normal" now and is taught in Communications Departments at all liberal arts colleges. Not centering for the White gaze is to be expected from all BIPOC-made content—it's no longer the issue it was when we started making shows. Muslims are intertwined into all aspects of pop culture, and for the most part the narrative is being told in culturally competent ways. Muslims are intertwined into all aspects of American politics as well—Muslim elected officials exist in all levels of civic society, and the Muslim vote is significantly wooed during major election cycles.

I often wonder if our podcast made a significant shift in culture, changing how Muslims get to exist in society. Did it work? Did that one Muslim girl in the middle of Nebraska feel more empowered now than she did before she heard our podcast? Did we help change the brains of people in the middle of the country who had no access to a Muslim? Did us telling our story of how we exist as Muslim women help make a cultural mark on how society behaves now?

The thing about shifting culture is that it's so subtle it doesn't feel like a big win. Because the whole point of shifting culture is to make the culture accept a new normal. The goalpost keeps shifting, and you keep pushing for progressive change.

But that's how shifting political paradigms works—we are changing perspectives of reality. Culture is always shifting—you just have to listen closely for it.

Culture is always shifting—you just have to listen closely for it.

A Love Offering to Miami's Black Past, Present, and Future

Nadege Green

Nadege Green (she/her) is a researcher, writer, community archivist, and audio producer based in Miami. Her work centers the lived experiences of Black people in south Florida. Her practice and approach to storytelling is deeply rooted in history and first-person narratives. She is the founder of Black Miami-Dade, a history and creative studio that resists the erasure of Miami-Dade's Black past. Her reporting has appeared on NPR, WLRN News, Marketplace, and in *The Atlantic*. Nadege is a frequent lecturer and speaker in academic and community settings around disparities in Miami-Dade, community storytelling, local history, and race. A child of Haitian immigrants and former farmworkers, she was born and raised in the county of Dade.

When I go to community settings in Miami to talk about local Black history, I usually ask the audience to raise their hands if they've ever heard of the Montgomery bus boycott—nearly every hand goes up. I then say, "Keep your hands up if you can tell me about desegregating Miami-Dade transit buses." Nearly every hand falls.

Long before Florida started its attacks on teaching meaningful Black history in our schools, we were already failing at teaching local Black history. There are few accessible materials on Miami's Black history designed for younger readers and for educators who want printable resources in the K-12 school system and elsewhere.

I created Black Miami-Dade, a history and storytelling platform, to resist the erasure of Miami's Black past. One of the first things I did was commission Miami artist Chris Friday to make coloring pages that corresponded with the research on Miami's Black history. For example, Miami could not become a city without the Black men who signed the city's incorporation papers in 1896—44 percent of the people who signed were Black men. There are no photos of that day in 1896, but in a coloring page we visualize what these Black men could have looked like as they made Miami a city.

I am continuing to build out a body of free coloring pages about Miami's Black history that provides short and impactful moments in local Black history—and that of course invites the person coloring to envision and remember Miami's Black past with beautiful colors. Through exhibits, cultural programming, and community memory work, Black Miami-Dade is a love offering to Miami's Black past, present, and future.

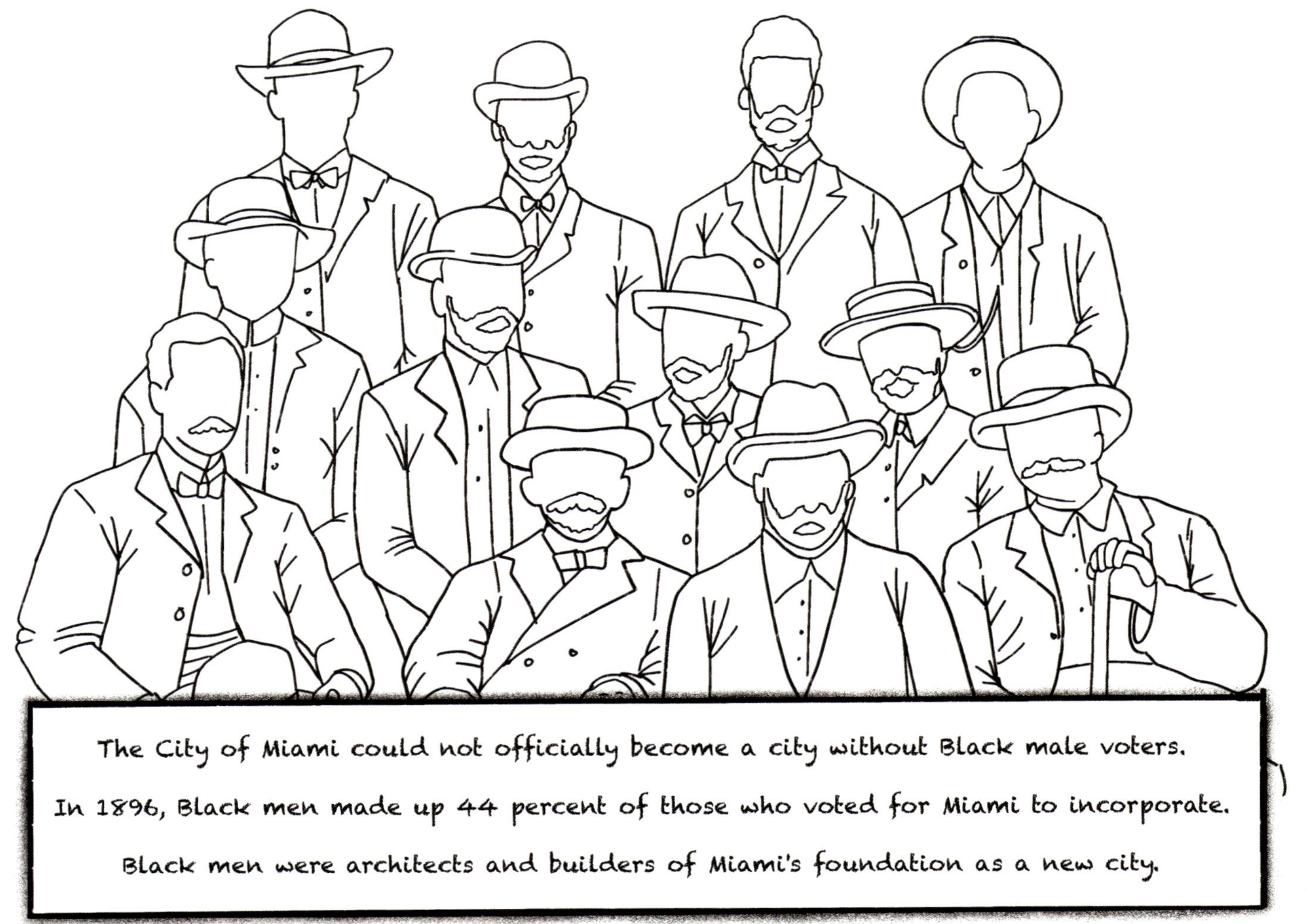

Illustration by Chris Friday for Black Miami-Dade. Free to reprint for noncommercial use. Find more Black Miami-Dade history at blackmiamidade.com

Miami
was officially incorporated in 1896.
The first name on the charter of the City of Miami is
Silas Austin,
a Black man.
Forty - four percent of the men who voted to incorporate the City of Miami were Black men.
Another Black man, ALEX LIGHTBOURNE gave a speech in favor of incorporation at the signing.
Illustration by Chris Friday for Black Miami-Dade. Free to reprint for noncommercial use. Find more Black Miami-Dade history at blackmiamidade.com

It’s Not Cool to Have a Racist High School Mascot

Akilah Hughes

(in conversation with Sangita Shresthova)

Akilah Hughes (she/her) is a writer, comedian, and YouTuber based in Brooklyn. A Crooked Media contributor and Sundance fellow, Akilah has had work featured on HBO, Netflix, MTV, Splinter, HuffPost, Paramount Network, and more. Her book of essays, *Obviously*, was published by Razorbill in 2019.

I think mascots—particularly high school mascots—matter. So much growing up takes place in high school. I often revisit who I was when I was younger and how I became the person I am now. I think this might be particularly true for millennials: We were the first generation that had cell phones in high schools. We were texting. The internet went from being a few websites that took two minutes to load to social media that is affecting elections, genocide, terrorism, and antiscience, antivaccine hysteria.

This is why I created a podcast. I want to rally my high school community around the idea of changing a racist mascot that is outdated, one that the school has already agreed needs to change. The Washington Redskins are now the Commanders, the Cleveland Indians are now the Guardians. Things are changing on a bigger scale. My thought process was, "Why not fight this on a smaller scale?" If we can effect positive change, why wouldn't we?

I've done dozens of interviews for this project. I spoke with people who create mascots. I spoke to the guy who created Gritty for the Philadelphia Flyers. I spoke with a woman in her seventies who physically makes the mascot costumes for professional teams. I've spoken with students and parents of students who currently go to my high school, which is really where this story begins for me.

The Beginning

I'm from Kentucky, and I am Black. I went to Boone County High School in Florence, Kentucky, in the shadow of 9/11. I was super involved—I did speech and drama, I was on the yearbook staff, I was on student council, I was in choir—and still there was this weird dichotomy. I competed on weekends in speech and drama tournaments, and we would win. And our school mascot was racist. It was a Confederate general named Mr. Rebel.

It really affects how I look back at my high school years. High school influenced what I wanted to do with my life, and yet I still refuse to wear a T-shirt with Mr. Rebel on it. I have hoodies and other apparel that still feature him, and I am ashamed to display them. It is akin to having a Klan robe in my closet. When I told people in other places about the reality of my high school, I learned that my experience was shocking to most people who didn't grow up in my small-minded community.

Boone County was not a super diverse school when I attended. There were probably around two thousand kids in the high school, and it was the biggest school in the area at the time. There were a couple dozen Black students, including me. On a typical day, I might see two other Black students in a class. I would often find myself counting the Black kids. Then I would see other Black kids counting the Black kids too because there were just so few of us.

Historically, Boone County in northern Kentucky is unique. It's where the South meets the North. It's right beneath the Ohio River, which runs into the Mississippi River. Literally, the line to freedom is that river. It's twenty minutes away by car. Boone County had several lynchings after the Civil War. The Klan held parades in the '20s. In the '90s, Boone County cops were caught on tape doing racist skits at an all-white police campout. There was a cross burned on a Black family's lawn in 2004. We had a football coach who was—somewhat ironically—named George Floyd. We called him Coach Floyd. He had been in the NFL. He was well-liked throughout the school, but there was an incident in which his office was destroyed. His computer was demolished. Someone spray-painted racial slurs on the walls. It was a shameful time in my adolescence.

If we can effect positive change, why wouldn't we?

Not Leaving High School Behind

After high school, I went to Berea College in Kentucky, which was the first Southern college to graduate Black students alongside white students before the end of the Civil War. Because of this, in 1904, the school was named in a state lawsuit that sought to segregate the schools. Berea lost and appealed the decision, and in 1908 the fight was taken to the Supreme Court. The highest court in the land agreed with the states and allowed states to require segregation at private schools.

Berea College is very cool. Case in point: it's also the alma mater of Carter G. Woodson, the guy who created Black History Week, which went on to become Black History Month. bell hooks was the writer in residence when I was enrolled there. I was lucky to talk with her often about race in America.

I graduated from Berea College in 2010. The ten-year reunion for my high school was in 2015. At this point, I was in New York and writing for the website Fusion, a joint venture between Univision and ABC. My beat was pop culture. Right after Dylann Roof went to a church in Charleston and murdered nine churchgoers, I found myself on a plane, heading to my high school reunion. I read his manifesto from my window seat. It was filled with Confederate flags, Confederate imagery—all the stuff that I remembered from high school.

Right then and there, I had this come-to-Jesus moment. I asked myself, "Why am I going back here? What about this place is worth revisiting?" There were Confederate flags on people's bumper stickers. The same flag from the manifesto would be tattooed on arms and printed on T-shirts. I remember having discussions about it in high school and how they would end with, "Well, I guess it represents pride *and* prejudice. Oh, well." But no. As a Black person who went to this high school, it is not only offensive; it is inherently violent. The Confederates are people who fought to keep my people enslaved, raped, without rights, and seen as less than human.

So, I went back to the reunion, and, to my surprise, everyone was lovely. I don't think that other Black people attended, but there were a lot of white kids who had grown up who, by that point, already had ten-year-old kids. A lot of them stayed in Kentucky and had kids right after high school, and some told me things like, "I can't believe we would wear that stuff. It was so stupid." It seemed that most people had moved on. I wrote an article to that effect when I went back to New York.

The gist of the article was "Confederate pride is a little bit hard to take, but thankfully, the kids that I went to school with have moved past it. I think all we need is for the country to grow up." The *Cincinnati Enquirer*, which is the biggest paper in the region, asked to rerun the article in the Sunday paper. And they did. They ran it with a giant photo of me superimposed on a Confederate flag, which caused a lot of tension in my hometown.

Everyone in Florence is still on Facebook, and there was a lot of online commentary, a lot of death threats, a lot of people saying that I was just a hater. I was even accused of being a loser in high school. And I don't know that I was super cool, but I definitely had friends in high school. If I had an ax to grind, it was against racism. I ended up saving one message on Facebook because it was so bizarre, "Boone County High School wasn't racist. I only got called the N word one time."

There is still much dissonance. On the one hand you hear things like, "We couldn't possibly be racist, but we hate this Black girl who said that we were. We don't hate her because she's Black, but just because she brought up racism." Many people just can't see their behavior in historical context. As educators, they don't even recognize that Kentucky was never in the Confederacy. To fight for a Confederate cause now is insane. On the other hand, there were many people—including teachers who worked at the school—who were like, "You're 100 percent correct. This is the stunted ass shit that we have to deal with every day when we go to work."

Confederate Legacies

In the early '90s, a couple in Kentucky funded the Mr. Rebel costume. Before they did this, there was no Mr. Rebel costume, but Confederate flags were everywhere because Boone County High School students were known as "the Rebels." The band was called the "Rebel Brigade." But mindlessly, they decided to have a guy in a costume be the mascot as a way to replace the Confederate flags. The couple that funded the costume wrote an op-ed in which they claimed I was wrong to point out the Rebel as racist. They claimed that the Rebel name was based on the film *Rebel Without a Cause*. I could not believe it. Like, we're looking at a Confederate general, an old white man, wearing gray and blue, with a sword on a horse. And you claim this is based on a 1950s movie starring James Dean as a young man? Obviously they had never seen *Rebel Without a Cause*!

I went to the library and spoke to a local historian. We went through the local newspapers from the 1950s where they're calling the school the Rebels before *Rebel Without a Cause* is even in production. Funny enough, a lot of schools in 1954—right at the beginning of integration in this country—either went private and became these segregation academies, so that they could still discriminate under the guise of, "Well, you can't have Black people come here because it's a private school, and no one's stopping us," or they adopted all this Confederate imagery to deter Black people. We've talked to a leading expert on all things Confederacy post–*Brown v. Board of Education*, Dr. Brandon Render, a history professor at the University of Utah, and he confirmed that much of the memory of the Confederacy was built during that time, as a way to deter integration.

The Past in the Present

In 2017 there was a white supremacist rally in Charlottesville. A woman, Heather Heyer, was killed by a guy who drove into a crowd of protesters. The guy wasn't old. He was a young man who grew up about ten minutes away from where I grew up. He went to Conner High School, another Boone County school. Suddenly, the media was scrutinizing how he was raised and how he was radicalized. Just a few months earlier, the principal at Boone County High School quietly got rid of the foam-headed Mr. Rebel mascot. The school announced that the students would be asked to rename the mascot. And there was little fanfare with the announcement that things would be changing. But then Charlottesville happened and suddenly the racists came out. Despite the announcement happening in the spring, the Save Mr. Rebel Facebook group launched in late August, just days after Charlottesville. The principal who decided to get rid of Mr. Rebel resigned in 2020.

Now there is a new principal, and there's been no movement in seven years since they said they're going to change the mascot. Currently there is no mascot. Boone County is just the concept "Rebels." This refusal to change presents the students with two options: racism or nothing. No mascot. When I interviewed students at homecoming this past year, they said emphatically that they have no school spirit. When they think of what it means to be a "rebel," they draw a blank. It is meaningless. To them, it's almost like the students are being punished. They complained, so now they don't get any mascot at all.

It's Time

This is where my podcast came in. Fourteen episodes have aired in conjunction with Ninth Planet Audio and iHeart Podcasts, starting in September 2024. Everyone involved with the school and community was forced to face themselves week after week after week. And while the show climbed the charts, it was made clear (through FOIA requests) that being exposed to an audience outside of their small community brought shame. My hope was that it would be an opportunity to bring the school together, to have them say, "This is what we stand for" and create a mascot that reflects something positive.

Locally, people have criticized me and said, "This is about you and it's going to hurt people's feelings," but I know why I am doing this (the mascot hasn't yet changed, and we intend to continue forcing this issue). I am doing this because change feels so slow there, and no one is asking what can be done about it. I want my podcast to light a fire to help them realize that we're not going away. We were there for homecoming. We were there for the school board meeting in December. We are making this podcast. When I interviewed people in December 2023, there was real fear. Clearly some emails were being sent.

Ultimately, my podcast reveals the level of disconnect and the lengths to which people will go to avoid being honest and open. It has been interesting, just seeing the groupings and alliances people form in an effort to look good publicly.

The principal assured me this is something the school cares about. Apparently, committees have to be formed and processes have to be established. Well, I am going to use this podcast to keep the pressure on. I am going to make the issue too hard to ignore. I am going to make it harder for them to just move on from this without enacting real change.

It's not my fault if they're ashamed. I'm happy to be part of whatever it takes for them to stop oppressing Black students. I'm willing to do it. I'm also not afraid of them anymore. This is a story about a very specific place and culture, but ultimately if we can prove that change is possible there, then there is no reason why the rest of the country can't move forward too and create a new, inclusive legacy instead of just pretending to be the kind of people who want that.

I want my podcast to light a fire to help them realize that we're not going away.

Care Work in Open-Source Software

A Reflection on p5.js

Qianqian Ye

Qianqian (Q) Ye (she/they) is a Chinese artist, creative technologist, and educator based in Los Angeles. Trained as an architect, she creates digital, physical, and social spaces exploring issues around gender, immigrants, power, and technology. Their most recent collaborative project, *The Future of Memory*, was a recipient of the Mozilla Creative Media Award. At the Processing Foundation, Qianqian is the lead of p5.js, an open-source art and education platform that prioritizes access and diversity in learning to code, with more than five million users. She currently teaches creative coding at USC Media Arts + Practice and 3D art at Parsons School of Design.

Your software should just be a neutral product. Your feature list is not long enough. You don't fix bugs fast enough. Your releases are too slow. You need to scale faster. You are not technical enough to be here. You are investing your time and resources in unnecessary and unimportant matters. Your software is too political.

Working with open-source software is working with people. Open-source software—software with source code that anyone can view, use, modify, and distribute—often appears faceless, hiding the individuals behind it. However, behind every open-source project, there are real people with bodies and feelings. While much attention has been paid to the code aspects of open-source software development, little attention has been given to the importance of care work in sustaining the community.

The platform p5.js (https://p5js.org) is a JavaScript library that aims to make creative expression and coding on the web accessible and inclusive for artists, designers, educators, and beginners. It was initially created by Lauren Lee McCarthy when she was frustrated by the lack of diversity in the open-source world. She felt alone as a woman of color and wished for a space that was more welcoming to queer people, trans people, women, and people of color.

I became the lead of p5.js when we moved to a rotating leadership model. I learned to code through p5.js as a beginner. As an immigrant, nonbinary, person of color, nonnative speaker, I found that the care work in the p5.js community is what drew me closer to the project the most.

Care is the heartbeat that activates the p5.js project, and we believe that care is the foundation, not the ceiling, for open-source software. Care work can take different shapes at different times in different scales for different people.

We challenged the way we were told about how open-source software should be built. We asked the right questions because solutions won't matter if the questions are wrong:

- Do you see the human faces behind software when using it?
- How does the software make you feel?
- What other aspects beyond software could benefit from open sourcing?
- Can the concept of care itself be open-sourced?

- How can we take care of each other?
- How can we foster care and intimacy in online spaces, such as GitHub?
- Is the platform we use for software development accessible to all?
- How can we prioritize care, intention, and slowness over speed in our work?
- How do we create a safe and welcoming space for new contributors?
- How can we make the software and community accessible to disabled people?
- How do we empower contributors?
- How can we distribute financial support to a wider community of contributors without being in the capitalist framework?
- What are the steps we need to take to go from coding to caring?

Making new contributors feel welcome, safe, and comfortable is care work. We invite new contributors into the space with accessible onboarding documentation, skill sharing, peer mentoring, and friendship. Writing documentation is a core act of care. We use simple language, avoid technical jargon, and provide beginner-friendly examples and explanations.

Recognizing and highlighting all types of contributions, no matter how seemingly "small," is care work. Besides code, we recognize and document all forms of contributions (docs, designs, events, activism, and more!) in our README and release notes.

Since I started leading p5.js full-time, I thought I'd spend at least half of my hours working on the code. However, deadlines for grant applications for p5.js events, Zoom meetings with contributors, planning sessions with collaborators, and check-ins after conflicts started to fill up my calendar. The amount of energy, time, and emotional labor spent on noncode contributions is often overlooked. Meanwhile, the default model of unpaid, volunteer labor in the open-source space is perpetually problematic, creating barriers to access for those who can't afford to volunteer their time. We strongly believe that most of the work should be financially supported.

Setting boundaries and reminding contributors to take a break in order to avoid burnout is care work. The human bodies behind software could feel burned out, lost, or anxious. While timely communication seems vital for community building, there's no rush. Having to say no helped us clear our vision. In 2019, we made a collective decision that "p5.js will not add any new features except those that increase access (inclusion and accessibility)." When burnout is real, we need to focus on what's important for us.

Organizing in-person and online community gatherings is care work. We wanted to see the communities come together online and in the real world, so we

Our Focus on Access

At the 2019 Contributors Conference, p5.js made the commitment to only add new features that increase access (inclusion and accessibility). We will not accept feature requests that don't support these efforts. We commit to the work of acknowledging, dismantling, and preventing barriers. This means considering intersecting[1] experiences of diversity that can impact access and participation. These include alignments of gender, race, ethnicity, sexuality, language, location, et cetera. We center the needs of marginalized groups over the continued comfort of those privileged within the p5.js community. We are collectively exploring the meaning of access. We are learning how to practice and teach access. We choose to think of access through expansive, intersectional, and coalitionary frameworks. This commitment is part of the core values of p5.js outlined in our Community Statement.

P5.js access statement, at https://github.com/processing/p5.js/blob/main/contributor_docs/access.md.

organized p5.js Community Salon, p5.js Access Day, p5.js Contributor Conference, and Processing Community Day. We discussed topics like critical web accessibility, disability arts, access and community building, access via translation, data sovereignty plus community access, and many more. We hung out in gardens and touched grass.

Navigating conflicts and working through different opinions is care work. We open-sourced our community statement, access statement, and code of conduct, and we believe that they should be living documents that are constantly updated. While having guiding community documents like a code of conduct is significant, the true challenge lies in their enforcement with empathy and sensitivity. We need to have check-ins, to talk about feelings, mediate, follow up, confront toxic behaviors, and tend to the scars.

Decentralizing the decision-making and leadership model is care work. Interested active contributors can take the role of stewards. Highly engaged stewards can become maintainers with access to merge pull requests, a way for contributors to suggest changes to a code repository and take part in decision-making. It's impossible to build the open-source software we want following the lone-genius myth. It is dangerous to rely on one person to make decisions for a community. Can we open-source leadership? Can we make spaces for others to lead? Creators inevitably carry bias of their own, so when creating tools, it's especially important to have a diversity of perspectives.

I often find solace in the metaphor of a garden when reflecting on p5.js as an open-source software and community. Just like tending to plants requires attention, care, and nurturing, our software ecosystem thrives when we prioritize the contributors over "product" and value relationships over speed. I often hope going to p5.js GitHub repositories, which are used to make and manage changes to an application's source code, is like going to online picnics. I've come to realize that I want to work on software that not only is for creative expression but also connects me and others with tenderness.

Working with p5.js, I've learned that the true essence of open-source software lies not just in the lines of code we write but in the relationships we cultivate, the support we provide, and the care we extend to one another. It's a reminder that beyond the digital realm, we are a community of individuals who believe that we can create together with each other, get closer to each other.

(I open-sourced my research about care work in open-source software in this link: https://www.are.na/q-_/care-work-in-open-source-software)

This image reinterprets a GitHub contribution graph—a calendar of green squares marking days of coding activity—as a digital garden. Inspired by a conversation about "digital gardening," I used AI tools to generate this visual, where software contributions grow into a lush, organic space. Image courtesy of Harvey Moon.

Affective Underground

Who Are the Architects of Feeling?

Terry Marshall

Terry Marshall (he/him) is a first-generation American activist, artist, cultural producer, trickster, and creative entrepreneur. Born in Boston to parents who immigrated from Barbados, Terry is committed to harnessing the creativity and radical imagination of diverse Black communities for Black liberation. His creative practice involves using world-building and pan-Afrofuturism to create transformative experiences of liberation. As a creative entrepreneur and a member of the Intelligent Mischief creative studio, Terry develops innovative cultural projects that shift culture. As a third culture creative, his projects amplify perspectives and integrate vision in unique ways. Terry's work also involves bringing creativity and design to social justice organizing through visioning workshops, festivals, and speaking engagements. Terry is one of the founders of Urban Griots and a former Laundromat Project fellow.

Prelude

In 1999 on a freezing rainy December night, about fifty young Black and Brown people gathered inside an anarchist bookstore. The assortment of headz covered in dreads, fades, Bantu knots, and head wraps were attending the still-new Urban Griots open mic poetry event in Boston's South End neighborhood. Inside were the usual trappings of a spoken-word night: lit incense, kente cloths hanging from the walls, and red, black, and green candles along with refreshments engulfing the participants in a circle of late '90s "conscious" aesthetic wrappings. This was the fourth event in the new series, and its numbers had been steadily growing. On every third Sunday of the month one could rely on hearing an assortment of spoken word, raps, and beats with politically charged lyrics that addressed social issues. Black love and unity were also crowd favorites. In this regard, Urban Griots was not too different from all of the other spoken-word poetry events around town, but this night was about to lead to a break from that story.

When I stepped into Urban Griots that night, I had just gotten off a flight coming back from a two-month internship in Oakland, California, and, more immediately, from New York, where I had attended my cousin's funeral. I was one of the founders of Urban Griots and had only seen the first two events before I took off to the West Coast for sixty days. My concerns, like that of a parent with a newborn left in the care of others for the first time, went out the door once I saw how much Urban Griots had grown since I left. To be fair, my mind was occupied with the more pressing concerns of how I was going to translate the experience I had over those previous two weeks to my lyrical comrades, because the last leg of my internship found me in the streets of Seattle, Washington, during the "Battle of Seattle," the massive direct-action protest that brought together sixty thousand people to shut down the World Trade Organization (WTO) meeting and all of downtown Seattle. The media blackout of the protest made it seem to the rest of the nation like the protest was a quick blip. When I came home, no one had any idea what had happened in Seattle. To my twenty-two-year-old self this felt like the revolution was going on outside and most people didn't have a clue.

I navigated through the welcome-back sea of hugs, embraces, and hand daps to get to the front of the room to make the revolution's announcement. My fellow collective members, after hearing of my accounts, announced that I was going up next. It occurred to me that I didn't do poetry. I hadn't prepared any Saul Williams-esque fire spoken word, no bars to win them over to my message. That is when I thought back to when we created Urban Griots and why we made it an open mic. We wanted people to have the experience of having a voice, to feel that no matter the skill level or form of performance, they could have a space to "build" and engage in discourse with and learn from one another. With that in mind I just spoke in a soapbox kind of way, describing how the corporate/racist media was denying them access to images of the masses revolting in the streets. How the WTO was responsible for the crushing debt of many of the home countries of the people in the room that night. How the state on many levels decided to respond to the protest with officers that looked like something out of the movie *RoboCop*, tanks, and so much tear gas that at one point they ran out. I also spoke about how we had to make connections between these problematic international policies created by the WTO to the domestic policies that led to the conditions that caused the death of my cousin. I made the call for people to come out to the next protest being planned for Washington, DC, that spring for the IMF/World Bank protest.

When I finished speaking, about twenty-one people came up and signed up to be a part of the next action. From that point on we added a news section to the monthly programming. This is what separated Urban Griots from the rest of the Boston poetry scene. This is why we started Urban Griots: to put theory into practice.

ooo

This was a snapshot into the political cultural scene I have dubbed the "Affective Underground." A subcultural scene from 1998 to 2010 that stretched across the country, connecting political activists, cultural workers, and civic media enthusiasts who created culture, affect, and media to mobilize people for the purposes of movement building. I'm going to tell the story of how a collective in this scene created spaces as civic media to build what I call "aesthetic-affective architecture" in Boston that gave birth to a vibrant youth organizing movement, and draw lessons for how using cultural and aesthetic activism today can lay the groundwork for the success of our movements going forward to deliver justice in this world.

What I call the "Affective Underground" can be seen as the political underside/expression of the musical scenes/trends called neo-soul and backpackers within the hip-hop music industry. By the late '90s, corporate control of the music industry, hip-hop in particular, had become monopolistic. With the passing of the

Telecommunications Act of 1996, which shredded regulations that had been in place since the New Deal, consolidation of communication companies began to rapidly spread, which resulted in homogenized radio playlists, fewer avenues for local artists to be heard, and massive layoffs due to cost-cutting measures. For working artists this meant record labels squeezing more profits out of them through unfair record deals while having to make their career conform to a narrow range of ghettocentric, stereotypical musical actions.

This was the industry's neoliberal turn, and with it came a backlash led by hip-hop artists who managed to carve out some space for an alternative. This looked like the production collective Soulquarians developing the neo-soul sound with artists like Erykah Badu singing conscious lyrics and rocking an Afrobohemian style that came directly out of the fan communities that consumed this new sound. A strand of those communities were activists who were battling the effects of neoliberalism in their lives such as the rise of the carceral state, gentrification, and immigration issues. These fans and activists who used arts and culture as weapons in their battles against these issues are the people who make up the Affective Underground.

Act I

The root of this scene in Boston begins with the 1997 opening of the movie *Love Jones*. The film, a romantic comedy set in Chicago, starred an all–African American cast that included Larenz Tate, Nia Long, Isaiah Washington, Bill Bellamy, and Lisa Nicole Carson. The main characters frequented a spoken-word jazz club where a local poet (Larenz Tate) and a Gordon Parks–inspired photographer (Nia Long) meet and fall in love. The film was notable at the time for showing a more nuanced view of Black American life that was hip, funny, and bohemian, as juxtaposed with the "hood" films of the '90s like *Boyz in the Hood* and *Menace II Society*. *Love Jones* became a cultural event that sparked a renewed interest in spoken word across African America.

After *Love Jones*'s release, several spoken-word nights sprang up in Boston. Based in the cafeteria of Roxbury Community College (the only predominantly Black institution in the Northeast) was Afrocentrics, which advertised itself as "Boston's very own *Love Jones*" and was operated by Michael Curry (who would go on to become the head of the Boston NAACP chapter). Around this same time Vernon C. Robinson, known as VCR to most, began to create several spoken-word events, including his most widely known, Verbalization. This same year, Askia Muhammad Touré came to Boston to teach at UMass Boston. Touré, himself one of the founders of the 1960s Black arts movement, took an interest in the burgeoning local poetry scene.

With the help of UMass professor and Black Power advocate Tony Van Der Meer, Askia gathered many of the scene's young poets and conducted political education sessions with them. The result was a politicization of a number of key players in the local poetry scene. This gathering had a profound effect on VCR, who would go on to become the most prolific spoken-word event creator in the city. Even more events popped up, such as the Lizard Lounge in Cambridge, Professor Van Der Meer and Clemencia Lee's Ogunnaike Galleria in the South End, and the Blackout Collective's monthly spoken-word feature at the Piano Factory. These spaces and events rounded out the ecosystem of Boston's late 1990s and early 2000s local spoken-word scene that was vibrant and heavily influenced by Black Power and Afrocentrix sensibilities.

Act II

The context for how the collective behind Urban Griots entered this scene was created in 1998. That year a small group of students led by the student group SOUL (Students Organizing for Unity and Liberation) at Roxbury Community College began an on-campus protest that led to a successful occupation of the president's office, the first such action at a college in the city of Boston since 1968. After two days, the students won most of their demands. A few notable demands were expansion of a daycare center for children of students, more computers for the library, removal of surveillance cameras on the campus, and internet access. The students' direct action captured the hearts and eyes of the Boston progressive community. We were asked to show up at every progressive event, presented with awards for being outstanding activists, and even shared a stage with Cornel West at Harvard discussing the power of direct action.

For many of us in the group, the building occupation was our first action ever. We felt undeserving of all of the attention, especially since so much of it was because we were young activists. The late '90s were cast in a shadow of the collapse of the international Left and the rising tide of victory of neoliberalism. Looking back, I can now see that we were the recipients of the Left's anxiety about a drought of youth participation in social movements, so our wellspring of youth plus actions looked like an oasis in the desert of the Left's retreat. There were a number of activist and community groups engaged in different sets of activities, but there was no social movement on the scale of what was witnessed in the '60s and '70s. We, the Left, needed more people. We needed more young people.

This was particularly true within the conservative environment of Boston. We became obsessed with finding our peers. I along with others went out to other college campuses as representatives of SOUL in search of our counterparts. Up on the top of the hill that Tufts sits on, we found them in the form of our future comrades Seth Markle and Emery Wright, who were the founders of the Nia Project. The Nia Project was a Black youth development and community-building organization based in Somerville, Massachusetts. They engaged young people in a process of critically understanding their history and in specific community building and organizing campaigns in the Greater Boston area and St. Helena Island in South Carolina.

Soon after we formed a coalition called "Next Movement," an ode to a popular song by the hip-hop band The Roots and also us announcing that we represented the next wave in the long history of social justice struggles. We began to meet and have "building sessions," which ranged from attending each other's programs and conducting workshops to hanging out late into the night at house parties. We learned that we had a common intellectual interest in Paulo Freire's concept of *conscientization*. We often shared in our sessions how we each became "conscious" and got involved in "the movement."

We started to see a through line: Many in our generation had become politicized through a combination of life experiences and listening to hip-hop music. In the late '80s and early '90s conscious hip-hop was the number one selling rap music, and it shaped our views on the possibilities of conducting mass political education through culture work. We came across the documentary called *All Power to the People*, where we learned the story about how a spoken-word event called the Black House became a meeting point for Bobby Seale and Huey Newton (cofounders of the Black Panther Party) and a host of national Black Power leaders (such as Amiri Baraka, Kwame Ture, and H. Rap Brown) before they became infamous. We loved the idea of the Black House. Much like our building sessions, we needed an immersive social space to connect with our peers and move them to action. We saw this as a concrete way to build a larger movement beyond our small orgs and collectives.

Seth Markle and I met up at a café to hammer out this dream. We identified the spoken-word movement as an entry point, seeing how many of us were practitioners and fans of the genre and it was clearly where the cultural wave of attention was. We played around with some names, but the one that we thought was the best was Seth's favorite phrase from Michael Eric Dyson: Urban Griots (he coined this term to explain how modern-day rappers were connected to precolonial West African village storytellers). We talked about not wanting to put on just another event—we did not consider ourselves party promoters per se. We wanted to create an experience that resonated with folks of our generation and moved them to take action.

We weren't interested in recreating the '60s so much as we were interested in making sure the '90s and 2000s became iconic decades themselves. This made the space and location key. We chose the Lucy Parsons Center, the local anarchist bookshop and social center in the South End. Because I was a member of the collective, we got the space for free and had twenty-four-hour access. But what made Lucy Parsons a crucial pick was the books. The store was a two-story, makeshift structure with several large bookshelves on wheels that allowed us to bend the imaginary of the space to whatever we wanted. No other poetry joint was being held in a bookstore, let alone a radical one. The imagery of rows of young Black and Brown people sitting cross-legged on the floor surrounded by books and posters of iconic revolutionary figures from wall to wall was exactly the vision that arose from our media-saturated DIY conscious evolutionary minds.

The experience often went like this:

One would either receive a flyer (often thanks to the design skills of Aaron) or would hear about Urban Griots through word of mouth. The flyer design spoke to the rap backpacker-neo-soul aesthetic of the time with a revolutionary five-pointed star. When someone arrived at the location, they were greeted at the door with a small sheet of paper that laid out the purpose and principles of Urban Griots. People often expressed surprise that they hadn't known about the bookstore before and its impressive Black liberation section. At the event, there was food and an open mic sign-up sheet was passed around. We kept it an open mic so that folks could have a deeply democratic and participatory experience. We always ended with a "news" update on how to sign up for the latest protest or community group. We created an email list of participants so we could send thank-yous, announcements for the next event, and urgent actions. The Monday after an event, many folks would show up to patronize the bookstore.

We would give shoutouts to the other events in the poetry ecosystem. We would attend their nights, and they often would attend Urban Griots'. There was healthy communication between all of the spoken-word organizers. There was an unspoken rule that one tried not to have events on the same night. Some of the other events started to direct people to community actions and events as well.

My description in the prelude was an example of how we were able to recruit young Bostonians to join us in direct actions as a part of the antiglobalization movement. Participants wrote poems and told stories about the actions we took, which would pique the interest of others. We took vanloads of people from Boston to the "shutdowns" of multiple cities such as Washington, DC, for the IMF/World Bank Protest, the Philadelphia Republican National Convention shutdown, and the large protests in Boston at the Democratic primary debates to allow Green Party

I'm livin' in it
Breathin' in it
It's more than just F#Kim'*
Believin' in it

-DEAD PREZ, Police State

NEXT MOVEMENT

United front of youth of color groups and individuals fighting the police state apparatus. Mobilizing and educating youth of color for the freedom of Mumia Abu Jamal and all political prisoners

for more info contact : nextmovement51@hotmail.com

NIA PROJECT

Student run one on one mentoring program that links black college and high school students together . Focus is on education and community advocacy

for more info contact : niaproject@hotmail.com

SOUL

*S*tudents *O*rganizing for *U*nity & *L*iberation
Revolutionary youth organization working to build a peoples movement in the Greater Boston area. We focus on education & organization in the working class communities of color

for more info contact: soul_101@hotmail.com

ACT OUT

Revolutionary Young Sisters for Social Justice
Goal is to activate young women to do grass roots politcal organizing in their communities

for more info contact: kmurray@hotmail.com

RECONSTRUCTION

Collective of working class youth who use culture as a weapon in attaining liberation in this struggle. We provide a monthly venue for expression with no creative boundries that includes drumming, spoken word, free style, and visual art for the Hip Hop Nation

for more info contact: Urbangriot@excite.com

Flyer for Urban Griots that was used for every show, 1999–2002. Images courtesy of Seth Markle.

candidate Ralph Nader in. For the Boston action, Seth and I became activist reporters for the local Independent Media Center.

Next Movement and Urban Griots soon got the reputation of being the center point of radical youth activism in the city of Boston. Our months were busy: If you were a member of Streets Is Watching (SOUL transformed into the anti–police brutality collective), you were conducting anti–police brutality workshops at a Boston high school or youth program. If you were a member of the Nia Project, you were running an after-school youth program in Somerville for African American and Haitian American youth. All group members attended an Urban Griots planning meeting and would leave with assignments to prep for the event. You then would attend a national call/meeting for an antiglobalization shutdown action where you would have to figure out the logistics for your local affinity group to receive direct action training, rent a van, and set up lodging in the new city. Then the last Sunday of the month would roll around. We would set up the Lucy Parsons Center for the event, where we would hopefully recruit some new folks into the actions or the local programs we ran. The next month would begin and we would start all over again.

Flyer for the No More Prisons tour. The Boston show was a collaboration between Next Movement and No More Prisons, and was Dead Prez's first appearance in Boston, May 13, 2000. Images courtesy of Seth Markle.

Act III

Given this schedule and seeing that most of the groups in Next Movement were underfunded small collectives and Urban Griots was not funded at all (there was a charge of zero at the door), this level of activity could not last forever. Urban Griots lasted from 1999 to 2001. Attendance did not decline, and we never missed a Sunday. We decided to shut our doors on a high note because we began to feel the strains of keeping up an independent monthly event without resources. We were all running other programs or had day jobs while doing Urban Griots. Our political disagreements around the direction and nature of the national antiglobalization movement and our participation in it began to show. We questioned the effectiveness of the actions after Seattle's WTO protests and wondered if we were just running around from city to city getting arrested while depleting resources from the local programs that served our communities. We also did not have ideological cohesiveness over the purpose of Urban Griots. While some of us saw it in the tradition of Amílcar Cabral's quote "culture is a weapon," others wished for it to go down in size back to just ten of us having a get-together.

Urban Griots' impact should not be measured by the length of its existence. In its short time it had an outsized influence in not only the city of Boston but also nationally through two other Affective Underground formations.

Eric Wissa, who ran the youth program at the Cambridge American Friends Service Committee, started a youth open mic poetry event called Critical Breakdown. I worked next to Eric in the basement office of AFSC (where I gave the name Critical Breakdown to the event), and we would share tips on how to run events and youth programming. Critical Breakdown would go on to become the largest youth event in the city of Boston, period. It became the center of youth activism in Boston between 2002 and 2009, with thousands attending events and protests that were led by the organization. Eric said that Urban Griots was the inspiration for the direction of Critical Breakdown.

In 2002, twin lawyers, Carlton E. Williams and Christian A. Williams, started an underground party called Leftist Lounge. Most of the crew that helped start the first Leftist Lounge were former Urban Griots collective members. Leftist Lounge resembled a psychedelic underground revolutionary disco, where one would be soaked in sweat from dancing while being surrounded by larger-than-life photos of Angela Davis and Che Guevara. Leftist Lounge went on to grow to about ten chapters across the country that raised money for grassroots social justice organizations and served as imaginal spaces for activists to unwind. With Urban Griots, the power of experiential as a medium for social justice was just getting started.

Cultural movements are the world-building of the politics of our time.

I would like to end by sharing lessons I have learned from my experience in Urban Griots that I believe could help the organizers, cultural activists, and strategists of today effectively build the infrastructure to create cultural shifts to make the politics we desire:

- There is no silo between culture making and activism; we have to integrate culture into our political movements. Why? Culture and art have the ability to attract more people to our movements, those whom traditional politics may not appeal to. Applied culture making (applied culture) in this way is organized aesthetics, which engages people through their senses and emotions.
- Mobilize affect: How people feel matters. Putting affect on the table when activists are constructing strategy increases the effectiveness of our organizing. Feelings are often overlooked in our movements. At best, we mobilize fear and anger and we leave off the table hope, inspiration, beauty, and joy as motivating tools for transformation. We must take seriously Cornel West's quote: "Justice is what love looks like in public."
- World-building is a tool: Urban Griots was much more than a poetry night. Urban Griots was an *aesthetic* form that allowed us to spread ideas through the *affective* format of poetry and art, creating a structure (institution) to help facilitate a cultural shift. We used it to create a space that embodied the new world we fought for. That space became a portal to that new world. Words and ideas being expressed poetically in a space owned by the Left became a practice of that world. It is world-building. We can do more than protest. Urban Griots became a place to catalyze a person's political journey and political identity.

These are lessons that I and others in my creative studio, Intelligent Mischief, continue to apply today. We primarily engage in world-building through content creation and experience design. We also employ a strategy of scene building by participating in cultural scenes by holding artist gatherings and experientials. Within cultural scenes, participants are building mini worlds that embody their values and ideas. These scenes serve as the basic units of cultural movements, which go on to influence politics. Cultural movements are the world-building of the politics of our time. My hope is that you, the reader, can see your café or hair salon as more than just that. These spaces can be the infrastructure for the transformative experiences that we need to build new worlds.

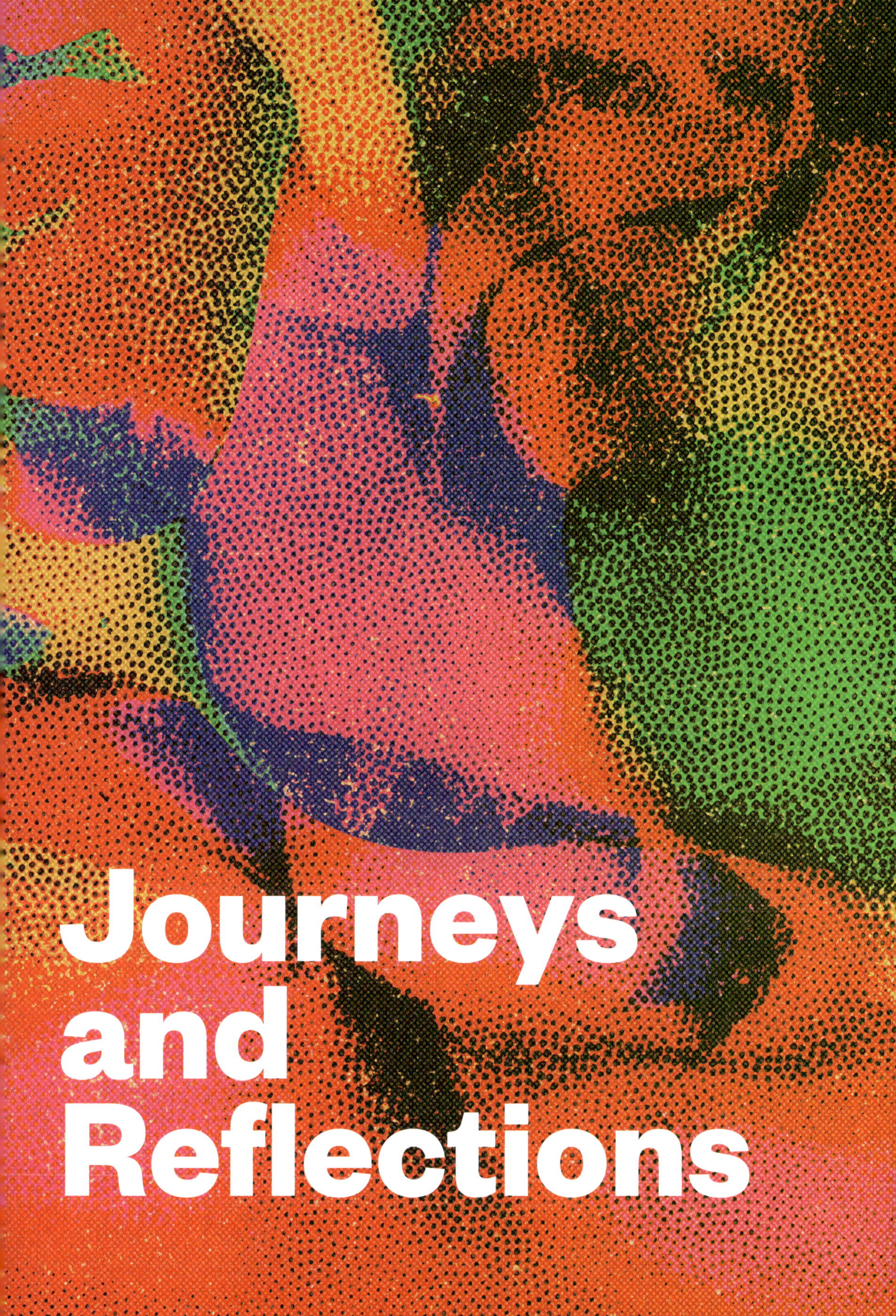

Journeys and Reflections

Awakening the Archives

A Search for Family, Connection, and Meaning

Arianne Edmonds

Arianne Edmonds (she/her) is a fifth-generation Angeleno, archivist, civic leader, and founder of the J. L. Edmonds Project, an initiative dedicated to preserving the history and culture of the Black American West. She has curated and presented her research about Black history, memory, and legacy at several cultural institutions around the United States. Her family archives stretch back to the 1850s, and her story as the keeper of her ancestral records can be found in *The New York Times 1619 Project*, *The Root*, and *LA Weekly*. Arianne graduated from University of the Arts in 2008, started her career in children's programming at Sesame Street Workshop, and spent the last decade focusing on community engagement, cultural strategy, and campaign development for brands, Fortune 500 companies, government agencies, and nonprofits. She was appointed commissioner of the Los Angeles Public Library in 2021.

The North Star of my life's work has been, and maybe always will be, chasing the stories of my great-great-grandfather, Jefferson Lewis Edmonds. Finding him helped me find my own story. Jefferson was born in October 1852 enslaved on the Edmonds Plantation in Crawford, Mississippi. After emancipation he would go on to become a teacher, farmer, real estate entrepreneur, and political activist. His most prized achievement was becoming the owner and editor of *The Liberator* newspaper, an early twentieth-century Los Angeles newspaper focused on the Black American experience. *The Liberator*, founded in 1900, covered local and international news, advocated for improved social and economic conditions for Black Angelenos, and was a champion for small business and women's rights. In many ways, *The Liberator* served as a civic media guide to help Black Americans transition out of the painful legacy of slavery and into their rights as citizens.

Jefferson saved each issue of *The Liberator* paper and bound them in a series of books. These books have been handed down in our family for over a hundred years. And in 2009, my dad handed the papers down to me. That's where our partnership began, Jefferson in spirit form, me earthbound. Together we altered the collective memory of the City of Angels and bent it toward the achievements, significance, and grace of the early Black Angeleno settlers.

I got really good at telling Jefferson's story, but it would take me nearly a decade to have the courage to start sharing my own. In the beginning I set out to make a name for Jefferson. I didn't want his work or his legacy to be forgotten. I wanted his efforts, his hopes, his vision to be etched in the walls of city hall. I was combating Black historical erasure, and I was doing it by force. However, slowly, gradually, and softly my efforts would shift from hero building to discovering the man, the father, the imperfections—and eventually learning about me.

Jefferson would spend a lifetime organizing rallies and town halls and hosting top Black thought leaders of the day. His goal: to help Black Angelenos feel worthy of a life so beautiful, so loving, so powerful, and so full. In the August 1913 California edition of *The Crisis* magazine, W. E. B. Du Bois wrote, "Los Angeles is wonderful. The air is scented with orange blossoms, and the beautiful homes lay low crowding on the earth as though they love its scents and flowers." He wrote this about his visit to Los Angeles on a guided city tour accompanied by Jefferson and his contemporaries, who were focused on showing Du Bois just how lovely life can be as a newly minted Black American citizen. The through line of all his social justice efforts was really to help define what Black citizenship should look like, how it should feel, how to embody a full American experience post slavery.

Jefferson was a futurist, a world-builder. He didn't write much about his time in the South. He would, however, reference the fact that he was born enslaved. He talked about being a husband, a father, and a man of faith. He never shied away from all the shadowy parts of his identity, but his gaze was continually fixed toward the road ahead. He cried out against injustice, but he also held tightly to joy. He was clear about his vision for Black liberation and the importance of a fulfilled civic life. In the messiness and oftentimes loneliness of that work he remained optimistic and kept hope as his guiding light. It would have been really easy for him to let his heart grow cold with all the challenges he faced. He had seen so much death, so much devastation. It's easy to let all that injustice and heartache choke up all your words and rob your humanity. Jefferson did the opposite. In 1906 he wrote in *The Liberator*, "The Negro must keep a stout heart. He must not be discouraged. The situation is bad enough, but it is not hopeless. If the Negro loses hope, then he can do nothing for himself, neither can anyone else do anything for him. Hold your head above the waves!"

The same man who authored fire-breathing op-eds about his fear of Jim Crow law making its way to Los Angeles, urging his readership to hold lawmakers accountable, was also filling the pages of *The Liberator* with stories about his family. He published his son's (my great-grandfather's) award-winning school essays and praised his daughter Susie for stepping up as assistant editor of the paper. For years, I focused almost entirely on his accomplishments, his footprint in the world. When I started my own family, I started to better understand just how much family fueled his life's purpose.

ooo

My journey starts off in solitude. I went searching, reading, and sifting through archival records. I was exploring and poring over documents, scrolling through microfiche, and looking at old photographs and periodicals. I became an investigator and an observer looking from the outside in. I was intent on understanding what secret strength supported Jefferson and his fight for Black sovereignty and wholeness. How was he able to dream and envision such a radically different life from the enslaved world that he was born into? I didn't just want to read about it. I wanted to feel that fire in my life too.

The Liberator

Devoted to the Cause of Good Governmentand the Advancement of the Afro-American.

VOL. VII. LOS ANGELES, CAL., JUNE 1905. No. 2

A Scene in Southern California

Your Spring Suit is Ready

You will be immensely pleased with the style and fine appearance of "F. B. Q." Spring Suits. We want you to come and see them whether or not you are ready to make a purchase.

CHAS. W. ENNIS, 233 S. Spring St.

The Liberator, vol. 7, no. 2, June 1905. Courtesy of the Edmonds Family Liberator Collection, Los Angeles Public Library.

Miss Brown Lays Out a Walking Delegate Page 5

THE LIBERATOR

A Weekly Newspaper Devoted to the Cause of Good Government and the Advancement of the Afro-Americans.

Vol. IX 5 cts. a copy LOS ANGELES, CAL., APRIL, 14, 1911 $1.50 a year No. 9

"DR. W. E. B. DU BOIS"

Dr. W. E. B. Du Bois will be one of the representatives of the United States to the Universal Race Congress at London, England, next July.

Dr. Du Bois is one of the most eminent scholars in this country. His contributions to the leading publications of the country are such that they create a surprise when his racial idedtity becomes known, which usually brings out the exclamation —"I did not know he was colored."

Dr. W. E. B. Du Bois

Prejudice Let Loose

The attitude of certain Southern newspapers in the recent Booker Washington affair is contemptible. They seemed to take particular delight in putting the worst possible construction upon every phase of the incident that seemed to be damaging to Mr. Washington. The high character of the man, the splendid services rendered by him in behalf of his race, the contributions he has made in every part of the country toward a better relation between the white people and the Negro—all that the man stands for was ignored and hurled aside, and the latent, lurking prejudice against the Negro came at once to the surface and once more asserted itself in tones of bitter hatred.

Then, when the explanations were made, and the plain, honest facts came out, completely clearing Mr. Washington of blame, as everybody who was free from prejudice and evil-wishing knew they would, these papers did not have the manliness to retract their miserable aspersions. They did nothing to repair the damage they had made to the reputation of a worthy man and upright citizen. Would they have treated a white man of the same high standing, wide reputation, and recognized helpful service in the same way? Never. They would not have dared to.

But good often comes out of trouble. Mr. Washington did not lack friends in his trying distress. They believed in him. And their unshaken confidence in him cheered his soul. Among these is the President of the United States, who sent him this letter:

"I am greatly distressed at your misfortune and I hasten to write you of my sympathy, my hope that you will soon recover from the wounds inflicted by insane suspicion or viciousness, and of my confidence in you, in your integrity and morality of character, and in your highest usefulness to your race and to all the people of this country.

"It would be a nation's loss if this untoward incident in any way impaired your great power for good in the solution of one of the most difficult problems before us.

"I want you to know that your friends are standing by you in every trial, and that I am proud to subscribe myself as one."

What Mr. Taft did for Mr. Washington in that letter was more by far in his favor than all that his traducers could do in their base efforts to fill the land with prejudice against him, his work and his race.—The Epworth Herald.

The Liberator, vol. 9, no. 9, April 14, 1911. Courtesy of the Edmonds Family Liberator Collection, Los Angeles Public Library.

I started sharing what I was finding. I did speaking engagements. I did conferences. I worked with historians and librarians and archivists to help piece together his story and share it with the public. Together with amazing collaborators, I created a curriculum for students and curated historical exhibitions. My family and I digitized *The Liberator* newspaper and parts of our family archive for students and researchers to have access. I was invited to fellowships and won awards and advised on archive projects nationally.

Over the years, with the help of friends and dear colleagues, my work began to shift outward, and I started helping others tell their own stories and explore their own ancestral connections. I began hosting interactive storytelling workshops with libraries and educational centers. As I was sharing Jefferson's story and his courageous decision to leave the South and move to Los Angeles to launch his newspaper, I would pause and ask audience members to join in. I'd ask things like, "Tell the person next to you about a time when you took a big risk. How did it go? What did you learn?" Some folks kept it cute and didn't go below the surface, but most didn't. Stories of leaving an abusive spouse, launching a business, and falling in love came up during our workshops.

Countless elders approached me after our workshops and shared that *The Liberator* had documented their family business or that the newspaper had helped them piece together a family story that they'd been wondering about. One woman showed me a picture of a little girl printed in *The Liberator* and told me it was her grandmother. She had never seen a photo of her that young. That feedback I kept getting helped to redefine the way I approached my work. I knew that my activated-history storytelling work needed to be more personal, but I was beginning to understand that it needed to feel communal and approachable. I needed to help connect the dots from the past and tell why these stories matter now.

The more I began talking about what I was learning from Jefferson and his social justice work, the more I was invited to share my story and my vision for Black America. Just as Jefferson stood before a Senate hearing in 1876 and testified about the violence he faced while registering Black voters after the passing of the Fifteenth Amendment, I too stood before the California Department of Justice and proclaimed that Black Americans deserve to receive reparations in this country. Together, although centuries apart, we spoke truth to power. We faced our lawmakers and demanded respect, justice, and humanity for Black Americans. What a gift he's offered me. What an honor it's been to get the chance to tell his story and slowly and softly start to interweave my own.

As the years passed, I got comfortable telling Jefferson's story side by side with my own. I slowly started to define my own voice and vision for Black citizenship,

THE LIBERATOR

A Weekly Newspaper Devoted to the Cause of Good Government and the Advancement of the American Negro

Vol. XI 5 cts. a copy LOS ANGELES, CAL., JAN. 17, 1913 $1.50 a year No. 13

NEGROES WHO HAVE MADE, AND ARE MAKING HISTORY

MR. PRIMUS HAYNES

Mr. Primus Haynes, of Lake Charles, Louisiana, who is in this city on a visit to his son, A. J. Haynes, is a member of a group of men who won imperishable renown in that tragic period of the Nation's history known as the Civil War. When the black phalanx was marching to the martial tune of "We Are Coming, Father Abraham; Two Hundred thousand strong, in response to President Lincoln's call for colored volunteers, Mr. Haynes, then a young man, left a Louisiana plantation and joined the ranks of that loyal marching host.

He was transferred from the ranks to the Navy, and was one of the gallant men who manned Admiral Farragut's fleet at Vicksburg and Port Hudson, and helped to reduce the Confederate forts, wiping out the opposing fleets and made it possible for the "Father of the waters to again float unvexed to the ocean."

At the naval battle of Mobile Bay, with the gallant, fearless, Farragut, at his own request, lashed to the rigging of his flag ship, Mr. Haynes was among the brave men who, executing Farragut's orders, sent the rebel fleet to the bottom of the bay; thus completing the re-establishment of our naval authority over the face of the entire mighty deep.

Mr. Haynes left a Louisiana plantation in 1863 to help put down the rebellion and put in force everywhere the proclamation of Emancipation. Having assisted in freeing his people and re-establishing the National authority in the seceeding states, he returned to his home in Louisiana and for the past thirty years has been an employe of the Lock-Moore Lumber Co., of Lake Charles.

Mr. Haynes is a visitor of distinction and should be honored by our citizens, as his distinguished service to his race and nation deserves.

Mr. C. C. Flint.

Mr. C. C. Flint is not only the leading grocer in the city, but the pioneer in that business. His splendid success against heavy odds had much to do with the success of others who subsequently entered the business.

Mr. Flint is a public-spirited man and has always taken a deep interest in public affairs, especially those looking to the advancement of members of his race. He has already been prominently mentioned as candidate for councilman next year. He is universally popoular; this with the growing disposition on the part of the liberal white people to give the Negroes representation will make his election very probable.

J. B. LOVING, Adj. Genl of E. & W. H. K. of P.

Mr. J. B. Loving, owing to his long and honorable service as deputy sheriff, who has won the sobriquet of "Major" at the sheriff's office, has held the position of

The Liberator, vol. 9, no. 13, January 17, 1913. Courtesy of the Edmonds Family Liberator Collection, Los Angeles Public Library.

This motherhood journey has tethered me to my past and my future.

fullness, and peace. It was the devastation and sorrow I didn't know how to contend with. Living through the COVID-19 lockdown, separated from family and friends, exposed a different layer of my work. Up until that point, I could empathize with Jefferson as a descendant and feel connected to the powerful legacy he built for our family, our city, and our nation. However, I wasn't completely ready to embody the pain, the loneliness, the devastation he must have felt at various moments in his powerful and transformative life. He managed to fearlessly protect a hope for a better future for Black people in America despite the years of harassment and violations as a formerly enslaved person. The willpower he possessed allowed himself to dream, to yearn.

For so long, I didn't quite know how to process or explain those parts of him. Just as I could compartmentalize all these parts of my life, all my passions, my shadows, my conflicting and overlapping identities, into neat little boxes, I was doing the same for his story. I made him our hero, because Black Americans have so few nationally recognized heroes. I had a singular focus, and it was to make sure his vision was realized. It's a mighty mission. But I would learn that it was only a part of a whole.

When I had my daughter, I understood his mission in my bones—in my body. I could physically understand his pain, his unyielding pursuit of a better future. I could no longer organize his story or my life into these neat little compartments. Becoming a mother blew all that open. Staying in the right lanes was no longer possible. Bringing life into this world was one of the greatest things I've ever done. It unleashed a wildness, a rawness in me that no longer allowed me to view this work from a singular, flat, academic hero-building lens. Parenthood, family life, the beauty and the chaos, the loveless parts of me, the helplessness, the hope, the gratitude—all of it. A whole new love emerged. This motherhood journey has tethered me to my past and my future. I'm now part of a continuum, linking this legacy beyond me and my research.

Toward the end of Jefferson's life you find him grappling with his own legacy. More and more discriminatory laws and policies were being put into place in Los Angeles at the time of his passing. Jefferson's tone changed. He became disillusioned, hurt, biting with his words. He seemed to be questioning if his work meant anything. Had he made a difference? I think that's why I worked so hard to bring him out of the shadows. I wanted to help him rewrite his ending, offer him peace, some assurance.

In the end, it seems he wanted to be remembered for more than just his achievements. Countless newspapers wrote about his noble character, his integrity, and the power of his pen. A former Los Angeles mayor gave the eulogy at his funeral. He was celebrated and revered. But when you visit his tombstone, which rests in the

Woodlawn Cemetery in Santa Monica, California, just a few miles away from his home, it reads, "Jefferson Lewis Edmonds, Father." It doesn't say social justice warrior, farmer, or editor of *The Liberator* newspaper. In bold all-cap letters it states "FATHER."

Discovering this hit me.

He did all this for us: my dad, my grandpa, me, my sweet Adina, her kids.

For the rest of my life I'll be discovering and rediscovering the lessons of resilience and unconditional love through Jefferson's story. He still planted flowers despite all the barriers and all the isolation he felt being a caretaker of such a heavy dream. He still tended to his garden and showed others how to harvest and feed themselves along the way. At the same time, he lovingly constructed a civic media blueprint for me, my family, Black Angelenos then and now.

How could I ever repay him? How could I even get out from behind that shadow? I decided to get very quiet, close my eyes, and ask these questions. What whispered back to me was. . . . Enjoy your life. Enjoy your family. Enjoy your time together. Remember all of us loved you so much that we laid a foundation for you. We will show you how to do the same. You don't have to worry if it makes sense. It's been done before. You carry with you all of our plans. You aren't starting from scratch. Wait for us in the forest. Wait for us near the trees in your backyard, at the beach. Listen for us when you feel the breeze. We are always with you. Always. Always. Always.

J. L. EDMONDS

Courtesy of the Edmonds Family Liberator Collection, Los Angeles Public Library.

For the rest of my life I'll be discovering and rediscovering the lessons of resilience and unconditional love through Jefferson's story.

Making the Impossible Possible

Niki Franco

Niki Franco (she/they) is a Caribbean abolitionist community organizer, writer, and facilitator of spaces for collective study. Seeking to disrupt the bureaucratic frameworks of academia and transactional ways relationships exist under capitalism, her work experiments with truth telling, radical history, and revolutionary imagination. Niki is also the host of the podcast *Getting to the Root of It with Venus Roots*.

The State Department stands
And all your coup d'etats have met success;
They caused this great uproar
Who's the real ambassador
Yeah, the real ambassador?

Who's the real ambassador?
It is evident we represent American society

Noted for its etiquette, its manners and sobriety
We have followed protocol with absolute propriety
We're Yankees to the core!

—Louis Armstrong, "The Real Ambassadors"

It's an early morning in early December 2018, the air is sticky and humid, palm trees sway in a pulsing beat, and businesses are adorned with vibrant pastel colors and hand-painted lettering. In Little Haiti, Miami, a group of us have prepared a counter art exhibition for Art Basel and Miami Art Week, typically a spectacle event where wealthy art collectors and celebrities flock to Miami for a cosplay of culture. The exhibition *2040: Travel to the Edge of a Dying World* was an immersive portal into imagining what the climate catastrophe of corporate greed and imperialism would result in by the year 2040, with a devastating impact on cities like Miami. Making meaning of what the future would hold for Black and Brown communities, (F)empower MIA, a Black and Brown QTBIPOC art collective, set out to create a postapocalyptic world, with an (un)futuristic fashion presentation illustrating the last generation in a dying world dressed in whatever materials and fabrics remain, films showcasing the climactic impact, an exhibition of multidisciplinary works by several (F)empower artist members, sonic landscapes weaving together revolutionary speeches and electronic production, and a panel discussion focused on preserving and utilizing ancestral farming and gardening techniques to counter food crises.

Today, and particularly since the summer of 2020 and its fervent protests and other mass political actions, many artists of color and other oppressed identities have eagerly begun collaborating with corporations and attaching their personal identity to brand campaigns. While representation and diversity in storytelling and cultural production are incredibly important, the trend of artists becoming ambassadors for brands illuminates the contradictions of the limits of identity politics and what is at stake when we align ourselves with corporations or governments that do not actually represent our values; art does not exist in a neutral or apolitical vacuum. In the words of Black scholar Robin D. G. Kelley, "Elite capture, after all, is about turning oppression and its cure into a (neo)liberal commodity exchange where identities become capitalism's latest currency rather than the grounds for revolutionary transformation."[1]

There is a quote attributed to Mark Twain that goes something like, "History doesn't repeat itself, but it often rhymes." Exploiting artists' social capital is not the latest evolution of "inclusive" capitalism but rather muscle inherent to the machine of imperialism.

On Sunday, November 6, 1955, *The New York Times* published an article titled "United States Has Secret Sonic Weapon—Jazz." As the revolving door of twentieth-century history continued its spin, the infectious spirit of self-determination and anticolonial struggle waged by oppressed people the world over was becoming a pandemic in the eyes of the United States—a pandemic worth battling by any means necessary, using any tool at their disposal, even the seemingly innocuous and recently developing genre of jazz music. As countries across Africa, Asia, Latin America, and the Caribbean relentlessly sought to expel colonial rule and demanded their freedom and the right to their land, the US State Department employed a number of secret strategies to ensure US global domination was not jeopardized but rather expanded and crystalized. The United States was not only threatened by Third World nations (those unaligned with either the capitalist First World or the socialist Second World) asserting their right to pursue dignity, it was also intimidated by overtures from the increasingly powerful and influential Soviet Union to these same nations.

Just two months before this *New York Times* headline, fourteen-year-old Emmett Till was brutally lynched, shot in the head, and thrown into a river for allegedly grabbing and threatening a white woman in Money, Mississippi; his two white murderers were later acquitted by an all-white jury. Then, on December 1 of the same year, Rosa Parks was arrested for refusing to give up her seat to a white person in Montgomery, Alabama. The savagery and cruelty of the white supremacy, anti-Blackness, Jim Crow legislation, and segregation that defined the US legal

Art does not exist in a neutral or apolitical vacuum.

system, economy, and sociopolitical rationale were on full display on a global stage. The daily horrors experienced by Black folks in America were culminating in the growing grassroots organization, protest, and resistance across every corner of the country, in what would eventually be known to history as the civil rights movement.

In 1956, the US State Department, understanding the impact that artists (and specifically Black artists) have on both domestic and international culture and society, unveiled one of their new programs to desperately rescue their global credibility: the jazz ambassadors. According to the State Department, "In a time of dangerous tensions and heightened propaganda, the State Department set out to connect American Jazz artists directly to international artists and foreign audiences to share this music, confront false narratives, and improve the public image of the United States in light of racial tension and inequality. Beginning in 1956, the State Department sent American artists and Jazz Ambassadors abroad—as it still does today—understanding that Jazz evolved from and mirrors the diverse and imperfect fibers of American life and democracy."[2] This program co-opted the cultural and creative capital earned by Black jazz artists such as Louis Armstrong, Dizzy Gillespie, and Duke Ellington to exert American soft power across the globe, but in the Third World nations of Africa, whose self-determination was in direct contradiction to US interests, this was meant to cloak the undermining of the sovereignty of Black nations and Black people across the continent. Both at home and abroad, Black liberation movements were contrary to the logic of the American state and were being simultaneously battled using the opposite ends of this new weapon, these jazz ambassadors.

One of the most glaring examples of the dual use of these jazz musicians in the international interests of the United States was the November 1960 visit to the Congo by Louis Armstrong, paid for and organized by the US State Department. Armstrong's host during his stay was Larry Devlin, the CIA station chief who had been appointed to his position a mere ten days after the Congo gained its independence from its colonial ruler, Belgium, in July of that year. As Armstrong was paraded around the country both as an emblem of American prestige and as a counterexample to the international media–reported oppression of Black people domestically in the United States, the CIA was already plotting the demise of Patrice Lumumba, the new democratically elected leader of the Congo. In the same month that Devlin was hosting the famous trumpeter and his wife at fancy dinners in Leopoldville, the capital of this newly liberated nation, the CIA station chief received instructions from an agent ("Joe from Paris") who was relaying instructions from CIA headquarters that he was to effect the assassination of Lumumba, according to Devlin's personal memoir. Two months later, Lumumba would be dead and Armstrong would be back in the United States.

According to newly declassified CIA documents, "from 1960 to 1968, the CIA conducted a series of fast-paced, multifaceted covert action (CA) operations in the newly independent Republic of the Congo (the Democratic Republic of the Congo today) to *minimize communist influence in a strategically vital, resource-rich location in central Africa*. The overall program—the largest in the CIA's history up until then—comprised activities dealing with regime change, political action, propaganda, air and marine operations, and arms interdiction. . . . By the time the operations ended, CIA had spent nearly $12 million (over $80 million today) in accomplishing the Eisenhower, Kennedy, and Johnson administrations' objective of establishing a pro-Western leadership in the Congo" (italics added).[3]

It is a chilling irony that a Black jazz musician from New Orleans, who was mortified by the violence of segregation and racism back home in America, was unwittingly abetting a political actor invested in the destruction of the sovereignty of a newly founded democracy in an African country. Years later, Louis Armstrong codeveloped a jazz musical, *The Real Ambassadors*, where he reflected on his experiences as a US State jazz ambassador and the conflicting feelings he navigated in that political role.

But the sprawling tentacles of the US State Department's covert actions grabbed even famous and influential Black artists who held political convictions contrary to the imperialist motives of the United States and never would have knowingly agreed to be part of a US State Department program and pulled these artists into their machinations. In a note to her brother, Nina Simone, the famed and highly influential singer and pianist, referred to the United States as the "United Snakes of America," and in her memoir, when describing the topics of discussion within her social milieu, she wrote, "We never talked about men or clothes. . . . It was always Marx, Lenin and revolution—real girls' talk." Through numerous protest songs, interviews, and her connections to other radical activists and artists in her social circle, she made it irrefutably clear throughout her career that she did not align herself with the policy interests of America.

Despite this opposition to US foreign policy, in 1961, Simone and thirty-two other prominent Black artists in the United States, such as Langston Hughes and Lionel Hampton, were invited for a "cultural exchange" with African artists, hosted by the American Society of African Culture (AMSAC) in Nigeria, another key African country that had just gained its independence from colonial rule the year prior. The 1961 Festival of Negro Art and Culture in Africa and America was meant to explore the "relationship between the culture and art of Africa and the Americas."[4] At face value, this trip postured itself as a unique opportunity for international exchange and learning. But after Nina Simone's death, it was revealed that AMSAC was actually secretly funded by the CIA—the same CIA that was simultaneously working on actively destabilizing Black Power movements abroad while its domestic partner, the FBI, was waging the same war at home with its now-famous campaign, COINTELPRO. As in the Louis Armstrong tour to Africa, artists were a Trojan horse to gain access to the hearts and minds (and natural resources) of newly independent countries without setting off too many alarms.

One of AMSAC's founders, John A. Davis, wrote in 1962, "If we fail . . . the world has taken one more step toward disorder and destruction." We can read between the lines and infer that the disorder and destruction he was most likely referring to was of anticolonial conflict and a deepening of Cold War animosities, yet in the eyes of the clandestine organization funding AMSAC, the CIA, this disorder and destruction would be better understood as a newly independent African country that does not fall in line with US hegemony and could potentially even ally itself with the Soviets. It is disturbing to learn that the American government deceived artists in innumerable ways, and it should raise questions as to how the elite (be it the US government or corporations) continue to find subtle strategies to undermine liberation, especially when done with the collaboration of artists of color.

What could it look like to use art to transform the social conditions under which imperial foreign policy is enacted? A historical example from the second half of the twentieth century is OSPAAAL, the Organization of Solidarity of the Peoples of Asia, Africa, and Latin America. While the United States was playing tricks on some of the most notable Black artists at home, OSPAAAL was conceived of and formally created in 1966 in Havana, Cuba, after the Tricontinental Conference, a meeting of more than five hundred delegates and two hundred observers from over eighty-two countries coming together to discuss anticolonial issues. The OSPAAAL posters became an international language of oppressed people all over the world. In fact, the 1960s and '70s oozed with radical, politically clear art created by people of color all across the United States, as well as the globe, and OSPAAAL is just one example of this effective weaponization of art against imperialism.

Emory Douglas, the former minister of culture of the Black Panther Party who was responsible for the visually arresting illustrations included in the Black Panther Party's newspaper (which became global iconography), wrote his own political artist manifesto where he lists twelve points for artists to think soberly about with regard to how impactful their art is. Number four on Douglas's list reads, "Recognize that art is a powerful tool, a language that can be used to enlighten, inform and guide to action." Number five on the list says, "Create art that Recognizes the Oppression of Others, and considers basic quality of life concerns and basic human rights issues."[5]

With Douglas's words in mind, it is a crisis of imagination to believe that there are no alternatives, that there are no other ways of navigating art-making in the United States. While of course the resources that are publicly available for artists and cultural workers are limited, there is a diverse web of inspiring models of co-ops, art collectives, and resource sharing with which we must reckon. From 2017 to 2022, my comrades and I operated as the QTBIPOC art collective (F)empower MIA, based in Miami, Florida—a city that many community organizers refer to as a "nonnegotiable battleground" and "ground zero" for fascist policies and anti-Black, anti-immigrant,

What could it look like to use art to transform the social conditions under which imperial foreign policy is enacted?

and anti-LGBTQIA policies. Over those years, we hosted numerous art exhibitions, installations, panel discussions, guerrilla-style activations, a community garden, book clubs, parties, and political boot camps to better equip ourselves for the responsibility of what it means to make art in a deeply unequal society, and we sowed the seeds of countless dreams of liberation as a result. We attempted to treat every sector of life and society as a terrain for struggle. It was deeply transformative to do this independent of corporate funding or museum trustees or a CEO; in many ways we felt uncompromised and free to bring some of our boldest visions to life.

Throughout this time, I spent many days of my weeks scouring archival posters and political theory texts and building relationships and recruiting new members to our collective. I am a first-generation immigrant whose family lineage is rooted in the Caribbean, and I grew up with the effects of imperialism, colonialism, and American exceptionalism, but producing revolutionary culture alongside friends made me believe a new world was possible.

Making mistakes, experimenting, and building anew are some of the best parts of being an artist—a process that has challenged me beyond my own individualistic aspirations to consider the implications of what art I create, for whom, and alongside whom. I would say these moments brought me and my comrades closer to our humanity, our fuller sense of self. As Toni Morrison has declared, "All good art is political. There is none that isn't. And the ones that try hard not to be political are political by saying, 'we love the status quo.'"[6]

Notes

Epigraph: Lyrics from "The Real Ambassadors," as performed by Louis Armstrong. Music by David Brubeck, and lyrics by David Brubeck and Iola Brubeck, 1962. Copyright © Derry Music Company. Reprinted with permission.

1 Robin D. G. Kelley, review of *Elite Capture: How the Powerful Took Over Identity Politics (And Everything Else)*, by Olúfẹ́mi O. Táíwò, accessed February 11, 2026, at https://www.haymarketbooks.org/books/1867-elite-capture.

2 Sunsariay Cox and J. P. Jenks, "Jazz Diplomacy: Then and Now," *DipNote*, April 30, 2021, https://2021-2025.state.gov/dipnote-u-s-department-of-state-official-blog/jazz-diplomacy-then-and-now.

3 David Robarge, "CIA's Covert Operations in the Congo, 1960–1968: Insights from Newly Declassified Documents," *Studies in Intelligence* 58, no. 3 (September 2014): 1–9, https://www.cia.gov/resources/csi/static/CIAs-Covert-Ops-Congo.pdf

4 "Opening of AMSAC's West African Cultural Center in Lagos to Be Marked by International 'Gifts of Art' Celebration," *AMSAC Newsletter* 4, no. 2 (1961): 1–2, 1. As cited at https://www.tandfonline.com/doi/full/10.1080/14794012.2018.1423601#d1e131.

5 Emory Douglas, POLITICAL ARTIST MANIFESTO: (Food for thought). Linked from https://www.moma.org/magazine/articles/642 at https://www.moma.org/d/pdfs/W1siZiIsIjIwMjEvMTAvMTMvMnYzcDk1MzVuc19FbW9yeV9Eb3VnbGFzX1BvbGl0aWNhbF9BcnRpc3RfTWFuaWZlc3RvLnBkZiJdXQ/Emory-Douglas_Political-Artist-Manifesto.pdf?sha=b60562e103f20e79

6 Kevin Nance, "The Spirit and the Strength: A Profile of Toni Morrison," *Poets & Writers Magazine* (November/December 2008), https://www.pw.org/content/the_spirit_and_the_strength_a_profile_of_toni_morrison.

The Lion and the Cobra

An Archive of Hope

Sydette Harry

Sydette Harry (she/her) is always a Far Rock first-generation Guyanese. She loves to ask questions that help us be as kind or as forceful as possible around media. She is slightly obsessed with information architecture, design, the difference between bias and context, AI, history, and performance studies. Previously community lead and editor at large at the Coral Project, she was most recently an editor at the Mozilla Foundation. Her writing has been in *The Rockaway Advocate*, *Foreign Policy Journal*, *Model View Culture*, and *Bitch*, and some of her presentations include the UN, TEDCivic, and Code for America. She is Blackamazon online. She'd rather be in the archives or the gym.

Encarta kickstarted my career.

Back when I was a little girl accessing the Encarta encyclopedia CD-ROM, I was fascinated by what the technology of "links" could do to expand learning history. Clicking links could guide you around knowledge and help you chronicle the steps you took in a world where learning was overwhelming. Guides, references, and bibliographies are catalogs and rules that bring order to the world.

I am grown up now—and Microsoft has stopped making Encarta—and I've learned that expanding our knowledge and connections within that knowledge is important and integral work to any civil society. And I've learned that trying to do so is one of the most heartbreaking things one can do. There is power in archives, and who is allowed to have that power is tightly controlled and connected to who has power in society. People who are not traditionally empowered often face huge resistance to adding to the official record. While social media and the internet age have often forged more paths to do so, they have also put up more obstacles. It has been a roller coaster.

We have to do it anyway.

The year before Encarta was released and ignited my love of links and archives, Sinéad O'Connor became famous by ripping up a photo of Pope John Paul II while a musical guest on *Saturday Night Live*. It was everywhere. I was vaguely aware of how mad it made people, including my uncle, a priest. What I also remember is how little anyone was willing to tell me, at eight years old, about *why* everyone was so mad, even while admitting Sinéad hadn't done anything but tell the truth and have an emotional response in public commensurate with discussing centuries of abuse in the Catholic Church. I was frustrated at not being able to look it up myself. It wasn't the first time and it wouldn't be the last, but that feeling of wanting to understand would stay with me. And then Microsoft Encarta came out.

I had always loved reading, especially encyclopedias, trivia books, and compendiums. I was fascinated not just by the facts but by how things were organized and who got to decide what went into books. It was a curiosity nurtured by my uncle, the very English priest. I also developed a lifelong irritation at who decided what knowledge was important and how people didn't see the links I did. My mother

Family photos of the author taken by Geraldine Harry circa 1991 (top) and 1993 (bottom), Far Rockaway, Queens.

would tell stories of how I would read six books at a time, furiously flipping between them like a baby detective, asking her why things she knew weren't in books. When we got Encarta in my house, she rejoiced, because the software reduced my incessant questions and gave her back her tables and living room floor.

I took it to college, where it intersected with my father's deportation and social media, building a blog, then a social following, then a career. It was all based on how people communicate and how the people consistently left out of making official archives could annotate, comment, and make change.

I organized to spread information around racism, organized for immigrant support, did public theater, and researched design on comment systems. I kept looking and failing, wondering how I could "make people listen." There had to be a way to share information and archive it, to "fix" things, to share information in new and different ways that used the power of the internet effectively. I was reaching a burnout point full of good intentions but little commitment to follow through on the missions that attracted me. My entire career had been an exercise in trying to find ways to fix this by linking communication to the creation of software, of art.

I believe information well conveyed is art. That is easy. The rest is hard.

After years of catching communications trends, UN speeches, fundraisers, and death threats, I found myself on *New York Times* bestseller lists, Stormfront hit lists, and both the mandatory follow and "can never be on our channel" lists in the news.

I was burnt. I was fried. "Listening to Black women" was a catchphrase, and DEI a trend, but still no one seemed ready to answer the questions. People were not listening. I was lauded for being "better than computers" at finding fake accounts and recognizing trolls, but still I was rejected for jobs and had TED Talks spiked on those topics for making people "uncomfortable." No matter how good I was, how much I cross-referenced and made links, I was not "allowed" to change knowledge on the level I felt it needed to be, not the way I wanted to. I needed some time to play with those links and reexamine them truly, so I threw out an all-points bulletin to my network and found the Civic Media Fellowship in 2019.

Then there was a pandemic, a summer of racial justice, and DEI pledges that grew from the summer of racial justice, and then a few short years later there were fewer Black people in media, technology. and philanthropy than when the pledges were made. We could be subjects of information but not the creators.

Bad information disconnected from reality becomes a war zone.

In March 2020 helicopters were flying over Highland Park, Los Angeles, and I am FaceTiming with my mother as she takes health walks past trucks filled with bodies in Far Rockaway, New York, at that point the COVID epicenter of the world. What do you do when your homes look like a war zone?

And as I watched it all happen, huddled with the world on community spaces creaking under the load, I realized that bad art is still art.

This information felt unnavigable. There was no art here, no guides. There wasn't something to "fix." It just was.

How I looked at archiving in the beginning—my own hubris—was as *hope*, and hope is a dangerous thing. Hope can power you to do incredible things and make you think your refusal to listen or consider others is admirable rather than self-centered. But you have to be egotistical to archive; you have to believe that what you think—not just about yourself but about the world—deserves to be heard not just by you but by worlds you will never be in.

My own journey into this practice came from blogging and social media. My father had been deported and I was angry. Armed with a recession and a freshly minted University of Pennsylvania degree, I had training, words, and time.

I also was looking for a community. Trying to bring words to experiences like deportation, sexual abuse, and racist abuse in public is always hard. I actually rediscovered Sinéad O'Connor as I got more and more public (and contentious) about discussing these things. At twenty-four years old, being told I was comparable to a rapist for challenging a feminist press's racism, or being accused of threatening murder for being willing to fight, O'Connor spoke to me. As I went from blogging to Tumblr, the ease of creation also led me to work even harder on cultivating things around a world I could imagine.

I was recognizing patterns, telling the truth, and building a community around it.

I also began to notice how annotating an archive, creating my own records, just enraged certain people. How it became an activity that wasn't seen as contributing to knowledge but a reason for planned, coordinated eradication. No one denied that these things were happening; they were just invested in either co-opting them or discrediting them until our voices were gone.

What I was noticing, along with many others, was the rise of Gamergate and the online Right. It became commonplace to see planned campaigns with fake Black people created to stir dissent pop up after major shootings in houses of worship, award shows, and elsewhere. These large-scale news events were followed up with calls to my home, people showing up at my retail job, calls to murder my friends. I had to know that I wasn't allowed to witness and write my own story safely. They controlled records and in disturbing their power—real or perceived—I was marking myself to be erased from the record.

I refused to be erased.

I was recognizing patterns, telling the truth, and building a community around it. Recording and reporting on these campaigns of hate became a group and social product. Hashtags and the camaraderie that came through them made tracking these things lighter. I wasn't alone. So many people worldwide were being harmed by hierarchical systems of oppression, nonrepresentative media, and the discounting of our experiences. Platforms may have been unaccountable to us but were (momentarily) being circumvented by our ability to build archives together in real time.

I became fascinated by information design, book design, comms. I led research on a platform for comments. I was convinced and hopeful that we could make software and journalism more like living archives. I believed that we were contributing to a more complete archive we could use later.

ooo

And then the pandemic comes.

There are photo spreads of field hospitals and refrigerated trucks outside my childhood home, where I learned to make links and love the books that had brought me to the Civic Media Fellowship.

I witness again journalists, academics, philanthropists—the people who pledged to listen, some of my professional peers—try to convince me that being close to something is not as useful as the guides and links I am so invested in.

I could produce things they could use, but I was magically—again—a subject, not an archivist. Even though that was my life, my home, and my work.

I am called, oddly enough, a banshee. Screaming and shredding icons. I tell more than one anchor of MSNBC how factually wrong they are about the resources where I live. I end another fellowship badly after the third time I was asked to support someone else for free, after they tacitly admit they hid behind me to justify someone else's budget. I am on panels with senators and receive ultimately facetious and exploitative "praise" for my bravery, as if bravery is the point instead of wanting the fields I had worked so hard professionally in to tell the truth about the place that made me, to tell fuller, better truths about what was being lost to protect the idea of people "doing enough."

I wanted them to acknowledge the bodies that had piled up inside my city, the fake Black internet accounts I had worked to uncover, at the risk of the corpse people threatened to make of my body for wanting to do so.

I thought of Sinéad; I used Wikipedia. I found out that there was almost the same amount of time between me discovering Encarta as a way to find out things and her ripping up the photo as there was between her ripping up the photo and the discovery of the 133 bodies of the women of the Magdalene Laundries in the middle of Dublin.

I think of how it is seldom mentioned that Sinéad O'Connor lived in the Magdalene Laundries. She was not just making a huge statement about the Catholic Church; she was also making a small one about a place she had called home and an even larger one about who was allowed to change the archives when it seemed the bodies were not enough.

ooo

My history degree let me know that my people—Black, immigrant, working class, Indigenous, and more—were less valued, but the pandemic showed that to a degree that I still have not recovered from. I ended up working on the evidence of it. I took my research and my fellowship, and I did a design sprint on how we could talk to people about COVID safety. I listened to people talk about how they lost children and about how they can't get information in the languages they speak.

I became a professional witness.

Archives and structures are, at their core, remembrances of witnessing. Rushing to find ways to remember, because we know we are already counting down to being gone. Graves are also archives, especially mass ones.

For me it was turning a mother talking about her dying children into a plea to translate important information into something besides English.

It's interviewing someone who is worried about losing their house and having a Zoom meeting with someone poolside in their new home tell you they won't ever really read the report you made from the worst moments in someone's life.

Watching the morgue trucks full of COVID victims disappear from my neighborhood with almost no words, even though the vaccine sites don't replace them, I think of what it would take to force remembrance. To confront the archives made. Who will make us wrestle with the gravity of everything? Who will be brave enough to tear the photos of icons, knowing the hell that's to come?

ooo

Now, as social media platforms crumble and things disappear, I've locked most of my prepandemic writing away for now. I don't know that I can approach it as an archivist. I cringe at myself a little, because I'm hiding history, the very thing I had worked all this time to avoid. I think of Sinéad O'Connor and her allegorical debut album *The Lion and the Cobra*.

I've dedicated a lot of my time since the fellowship to the civic. I've lectured (virtually) around the world, paneled with senators and the legal counsel of Wikipedia, and had my work referenced by the FTC.

I also read story after story of how, despite the big push of "listening," very little has changed in support of Black women in civic life, media, or tech. Many of my projects are shut down, and when I refuse to work for free or provide media moments, the support seems to shut down as well.

America has lost abortion rights, the very lack of which caused so many of the deaths in the Magdalene Laundries. So many of the same feminists who permitted Hugo Schwyzer to abuse me for their success are champions of creating "records" of this time.

I exchange sorrow and tears with activists who run clinics that are shutting down because when all is said and done, outside of the use of their "stories," it wasn't about them.

I am struggling with seeing the threads that connect things now and with ever feeling brave again after a pandemic, and a racial reckoning, and all of these moments of listening and witness that ultimately don't feel like anybody listened at all.

I think of the moment Sinéad rips that photo as an archive. An archive of who she was, of finding a new way to challenge the unchallenged figures and myths who built history, of taking what she knew of where she lived, of sharing and telling, of asking us to build something new.

I think of how she says in her book she never regrets it and how right now I don't either.

But if you ask if it was worth it?

If I still believe, if I still feel excited looking for the links and threads in the world?

I'm not sure. But I am again back on the floor looking for links, just like when I started.

The Place Where the Water Runs Among the Rocks

Mari Mari Narváez

Mari Mari Narváez (she/her) is a Puerto Rican journalist, writer, and human rights activist. She is the founder and executive director of Kilómetro Cero, a human rights organization that fights police violence and repression and proposes new forms of public safety, based on human rights and public health perspectives. Mari Mari has a master's degree in journalism and Latin American studies and has done doctoral work in history and gender studies. She is also a writer and columnist for various newspapers in Puerto Rico and the coauthor of six books in Spanish.

1

Nobody comes to seat us in this diner. I'm not offended. My hunger, which is menacing, is stronger than this cliché. I am my own route.[1] Upon passing the Wait to Be Seated sign, I look in the spacious room for our table. I take possession and deposit my belongings, and an unmasked woman approaches us. She offers to bring coffee. She's cordial, but something's off here. I take a good look around me and find a corridor of whiteness. We are out of place here, but not only because of our skin color, which is already secondary: We are the only ones wearing a mask, as recommended by the CDC in enclosed public places.

2

The Navajo people's culture is founded on their creation mythology. Diné Bahane,[2] which in Navajo means "the story of the people," is a legend recounting the origin of the earth with the sacred wind, "a mist of light that rose from the darkness to give life and purpose"[3] to the vastness. The physical realm of people did not yet exist, but the spiritual one did.

For the Navajo, there were three minor worlds before the current one. The first world was inhabited by "insect people." In the second and third worlds, the inhabitants lived in peace for a while, but then they began to fight among themselves and were expelled to a new world. In the fourth world, the first woman and man arose from the ears of corn. This cosmogonic mythology is similar to the Christian one. Early civilizations had cosmologies, worshiped an omnipotent creator or master spirit, believed in lesser supernatural entities, including evil gods who dealt disaster, suffering, and death. They also believed in the immortality of the human soul and the afterlife.

3

American progressives stop before Zoom panels begin in order to recognize and name the Indigenous tribes that inhabited the place where they are at that moment of the meeting. In my wildest days, I have told them that I do not need to go back to pre-Columbian times to recognize my colonized, exploited, wrecked situation. I tell them that I am Me, a Puerto Rican from Puerto Rico, the oldest colony in the world. "You must name your native tribes to acknowledge your colonial ancestry. I achieve the same just by naming myself."

Although Puerto Rico doesn't have self-government, culturally it is considered a nation as it has a distinct culture, history, language, and idiosyncrasies. I don't say this lightly. Since the United States of America invaded our country in 1898, both the English language and the US American culture have been imposed on this Spanish-speaking land in innumerable ways. When my father went to public school in the 1930s, it was mandatory for both faculty and students to speak English. He would always tell the stories of how absurd and almost surreal it was that his teachers, in Mayagüez, his hometown on the western side of the island, had to teach in a language they could barely speak. He used to say they would just shut the doors and speak Spanish, and if a high-ranking supervisor ever knocked on the door, everyone knew they had to pretend to be talking in "el difícil" (the hard one).

When I went to private school, that offensive was already proven to be a failure and useless due to the already historic, strong, cultural resistance of our people, so I didn't have to speak English. However, we did have to pledge allegiance to the United States flag every single morning of our lives. Most of us never understood why we had to exhibit a loyalty we did not feel. Maybe the United States was a respectable country like many others, but it wasn't ours, not politically, not culturally, not even emotionally. Puerto Rico is not "part" of the United States. It is a possession.[4]

The United States had political control of Puerto Rico because it received us as war booty from Spain and militarily invaded us in 1898. The United States was here illegally and immorally: Why did we have to pledge allegiance? Some of us, probably a small but loud minority that existed in most private schools, did not actually do it. Strategies were developed and explanations intentionally given out loud in order to recruit other members for the resistance. At least in my school, it worked brilliantly, but let's not get off the subject here.

To this day, the United States still has almost absolute control of our land, economy, government, and frontiers. Since the approval of the PROMESA Act in 2016, the United States even controls our budget. Our homeland, however, is the striking archipelago of Puerto Rico, "la Madre Isla" (the Mother Island), as Eugenio María de Hostos, "the Great Citizen of the Americas" and a national hero, named our main island, as opposed to "Madre Patria" (Mother Land), which is the name some people used in regard to Spain.

As a colonized country, American citizenship was imposed on us unilaterally.

Not because we didn't have Puerto Rican citizenship; we did and we still do.[5] We were given that passport so that the United States could use the cheap labor of our mostly Brown and Black people to draft us into their wars. We have been robbed of our lands for military purposes and have been guinea pigs for scientific and military experiments, from the use of napalm and other chemical weapons to the more than six decades of live ammunition practices around the civilian population of Vieques Island.

Our freedom fighters and anticolonialist leaders have been brutally repressed since the US invasion. That task was and indeed still is the reason the Puerto Rican police—the most corrupt and unaccountable among all US jurisdictions—was created.

Anyone who stood for any cause, even if it was an environmental or feminist cause, was oppressed and persecuted by the FBI's infamous COINTELPRO, a series of covert and illegal projects conducted by the FBI aimed at surveilling, infiltrating, discrediting, and disrupting political organizations and leaders. We've had hundreds of political prisoners, both on Puerto Rican land and in the United States. Puerto Rican revolutionaries have not only been incarcerated but also assassinated. The latest one, in 2005, was Filiberto Ojeda Ríos, the leader of the Ejército Popular Boricua-Macheteros.

Filiberto was larger than life. I was little when my parents talked to me about him. He fought to defend Puerto Rico's right to self-determination and independence, they said. He claimed his international right to use armed struggle to defend those rights in a colonial state.

One day he returned to Puerto Rico from prison with an electronic ankle bracelet, as his trial for the robbery of a Wells Fargo depot in Hartford, Connecticut—considered then the largest cash heist in US history—had been delayed. I was ten when my dad introduced me to him. Very few times, maybe never again, have I ever felt as astonished by someone's presence. On September 23, 1990, he took off his electronic tag and went underground.

Fifteen years later, in 2005, again on September 23, as thousands of us were returning from the commemoration of the Cry of Lares, the first major rebellion against Spanish rule in Puerto Rico, the FBI and the Puerto Rican police surrounded Filiberto's house in the western town of Hormigueros. Many of us took to the streets, some in front of the federal court in San Juan, while others went to Filiberto's neighborhood. Filiberto was killed that same day, left to bleed to death from a single shot to his lung. The FBI didn't let the doctors who showed up there give him first aid and didn't enter his house until the day after.

In the days that followed, it was obvious that something very deep and unsettling had happened in our country. Something had broken. Nobody seemed fearful to mourn Filiberto publicly. He was given the largest funeral in our history. Old men would do the military salute when the huge caravan escorting his coffin passed by. Teachers would bring children out from the schools to the streets, most of them raising construction paper machetes with their left arm to honor the late "machetero."

I know that I was changed that day. Having seen an army of FBI agents arrive at the island, surround a house, kill a man, then pick up their things and leave, like mercenaries, that day I learned, in real life, what colonialism was. And I was furious and disheartened, as so many were.

I didn't know what to do. I was drawn to do something violent, but I had never held a weapon in my hands. I don't know anything about using violence as a political mechanism, so I wrote. I insulted the FBI in mainstream media, I wrote about repression, and I began to question how we were all going to collectively retaliate for Filiberto's killing. I questioned myself on this topic for many years. And that is how I became fixated on state violence.

Years passed, and one day I began to document police use-of-force killings in Puerto Rico to gather data in what is known as a noncounting or nonrecording state: a state that does not record or count the information that is central to accountability because it doesn't have the minimum will to be accountable. I would tell myself: If they killed Filiberto Ojeda Ríos, who is a national hero, I am sure the police are killing other people. But who?

I founded Kilómetro Cero, a nonprofit organization that fights state violence and oppression and aspires to a Puerto Rico that protects human life, freedoms, and dignity. We have documented more than 120 police use-of-force deaths since 2014.

4

We Puerto Ricans from the archipelago are not really American citizens. To be a citizen is to be able to exercise all civic rights. We are colonial subjects with an American passport.[6] We cannot exercise all the rights of American citizenship, such as voting rights. But, more importantly, that citizenship was imposed by imperialism and colonization; thus, it is not a legitimate citizenship.

While our oppressor has responsibilities toward us as long as we are a colony because it holds all political and economic power, the solution to our oppression cannot reside in us becoming our oppressor. Colonialism is racist. Its only legacy is oppression. It is a supremacist act to frame Puerto Rico's oppression as

The solution to our oppression cannot reside in us becoming our oppressor.

a voting rights issue or as a "second-class citizenship" problem. It erases the history, the resistance, and the right of Puerto Ricans from this archipelago to exist as a nation. It perpetuates the narrative of our identity as Puerto Ricans as less than full "Americans." With that logic, we become empowered only by being fully incorporated into our oppressor—elevated only by becoming the colonizer. American citizenship is not superior to all other citizenships. The dignity of Puerto Ricans does not emanate from US citizenship. Our emancipation can only be achieved by supporting a dignified internationally compliant process of self-determination and decolonization.

5

I don't always go wild in those Zoom worlds. I must say that the people who fight in the United States teach me a lot. But yes, there's something about political correctness that always falls short. When you come from a place that has survived (have we?) an endless history of political violence, rather than being signs of solidarity and inclusion, as they are intended, these practices sometimes only accentuate the unnamed issues exploding in our faces every single day, that which exists and harms and dispossesses us on a daily basis but is not even mentioned, nevertheless acknowledged.

I remember *My Life Is My Sun Dance*, the book by Leonard Peltier, Sioux leader and former political prisoner, one of the most beloved books in my library. Our lives are a dance of resistance against our extinction. Today.

6

I always want to leave, and in that anxious restlessness, I don't stop long enough to think about where I'm going. But off you go. You make your plan, you juggle everything in order to be able to leave, you travel thousands of miles by plane, by car. You heed the cautionary notices. "Look, that area of the country is bad." "You haven't been to the United States since before the pandemic, and things have changed." "Look, that is the place where white supremacists put Trump in the presidency and they are armed, angry, and have impunity." "Beware of such a place, do not spend the night there, it is not good." "Better do this, look the other way, beware of solitary roads, and don't speak much." "When in doubt, look for larger cities, frequented hotels, not temporary stopovers." You listen and overcome all such sentiments, and you now must add a hatred against science and against the meager armies of timidly masked people in this country.

7

You arrive at your destination. The Navajo Nation is there, like you peeled off a very thin surface of skin from Arizona. Traversing two worlds at the same time: on one side, the white older men and women, perennially unmasked, who obstinately serve us in hotels, diners, and shops. On the other, the Navajo artisans and jewelers' stalls at the foot of the road, the markets and food stalls, the isolated, impoverished houses.

The Navajo boy, with his mask, shows us the Antelope Canyon, an unusual, kaleidoscopic, disconcerting natural landscape. This place must be unique in the world. In this wonder of a small, multicolored canyon, "the place where the water runs among the rocks," he takes the time to reveal to us something beyond the obvious, which is already a lot. He shows us the details, each extraordinary formation and its corresponding legend, each expressive corner, the places with the exact light, with the natural drawing for the photo ("What do you see there? . . . Look at the lion there. . . . See the bison forming over here. . . . Do not miss the seahorse").

While showing us the rock art, he takes us through the tremendous stories and legends that have been forged in this place that has existed for a little less than two hundred million years. The fact is that this entire region of canyons and red mountains with layers of rock and colorful cliffs is a spectacular record of the history of the earth, of its erosions, times, and metrics of life.

I must not leave without asking this pleasant and open guy a couple of questions. I can't come from so far away only to remain with my doubts, I think. So, with that perennial fear of risking each experience with a hyperpolitical stance, I ask him softly, as though in passing, about the use of the Navajo language and also about how his community has been able to keep control of such a rare, ravishing natural monument. The young man, who until now has been very animated and content, answers me without much drama, but also slightly changes his register. He tells me that fewer and fewer people in his community speak Navajo, that the youth speak primarily English. We chat briefly about how his nation has managed to maintain control of this rich and stunning place. We warm up when his tour is about to end and he has other people to attend to, but he finishes our exchange by telling me: "What they call Indigenous reservations here are really concentration camps."

I recognize myself in the naturalness of his tone change and in the spare drama he adopts when telling me what he just did, despite its harshness, its tragedy. The violence is so inherent that one seems to carry it inside, under a thin layer of skin that can easily peel off.

From a distance, he says goodbye to our group with a smile and the joy of having revealed great secrets during a formidable journey we might never experience again but will likely keep returning to. A place we will never be able to shed or forget.

Notes

1 "I am my own route" is the author's translation for "Yo misma fui mi ruta," a poem by Puerto Rican poet Julia de Burgos.

2 Joel Gladd, "Navajo Diné Bahane," *Anthology of Earlier American Literature* (College of Western Idaho), accessed October 25, 2023, https://cwi.pressbooks.pub/americanliterature/.

3 Wikipedia, "Mitología navajo," accessed October 25, 2023, https://es.wikipedia.org/wiki/Mitolog%C3%ADa_navajo.

4 Puerto Rico is a possession according to the Insular Cases, which refers to a series of Supreme Court decisions made beginning in 1901 concerning the constitutional rights afforded to residents of the overseas territories the United States had acquired in the Treaty of Paris: Puerto Rico, Guam, and the Philippines, as well as (eventually) the US Virgin Islands, American Samoa, and the Northern Mariana Islands. The Insular Cases are still largely in effect.

5 The author's father, Juan Mari Brás, was the first Puerto Rican to officially renounce his US citizenship, in 1994. After that, a chain of events led the Supreme Court of Puerto Rico to decide that Puerto Ricans have double citizenship: American and Puerto Rican, as we never lost the second one after the United States imposed its citizenship upon the island.

6 Jacqueline Font, "Puerto Ricans Are Hardly U.S. Citizens: They Are Colonial Subjects," Opinion, *Washington Post*, December 13, 2017, https://www.washingtonpost.com/opinions/puerto-ricans-are-hardly-us-citizens-they-are-colonial-subjects/2017/12/13/c0f1c700-de9f-11e7–89e8-edec16379010_story.html.

Design and Care

Dream, Rest, Play

Reflections on Designing Liberated Spaces for Black Women

Jennifer S. Roberts

Jennifer S. Roberts (she/her) is an interdisciplinary facilitator, artist, and social designer whose work over the last twenty years has been based in cocreation and design. Whether through coaching and consulting or hackathons and dream spaces, she aims to design immersive experiences that allow people to reimagine and redesign our communities for liberation. Her academic and artistic work taps into Afrofuturistic explorations designed by Black communities, particularly Black women. She is the cofounder of Building Utopia Deck, an Afrofuturism-based design toolkit, and the founder and executive director of Colored Girls Liberation Lab, an intergenerational healing and dream lab that aims to be a brave and protected space for Black women and femme-identifying people to design their most liberated lives in community. Jenn is a very proud graduate of Spelman College and lives in the DC area with her spunky and creative daughter.

What would the world be like if Black women had the opportunity to dream expansively? I've asked myself that question many times in my career and even more as of late. Overlapping systems of oppression and racism have kept Black women from having space to dream, rest, and play. As a result, we often must problem solve and build our communities from a place of lack and survival. While we acknowledge the importance of this ability to create a way out of no way, the work I've been exploring seeks to disrupt this culture, to give Black women a safe, brave, and protected space to reimagine freedom for themselves, their families, and communities.

Studies have shown that Black people are at a higher risk for depression and anxiety due to societal pressures, threats, and systemic racism. For Black women, our symptoms are often harder to identify and share with others because of the stigma of mental health in our communities. Microaggressions in our jobs and social interactions, layered on top of factors such as Superwoman syndrome, impact Black women disproportionately. We receive messages to be strong, to not rest, to bury our emotions, and to take on the burdens of our families and communities at our own expense.

As a Black woman working in education and nonprofits for the majority of my twenty-year professional journey, I've felt every type of pressure and slight. Even with a successful career, I often felt the need to hide portions of who I was or stifle my creativity and ideas to make others comfortable. Like many Black women, it took me years to heal and recover from my experiences in the workforce.

I have spent more than ten years helping organizations redesign their systems and workplaces for equity, and I have seen the freedom that comes with having space to reimagine. When given the time and space to reconsider and reflect on what has caused harm and then given the resources to dream up new solutions in community, creative paths forward are made. Outside of the workplace, I've seen the creative expansion that has come in my own personal time to reimagine. As I surveyed the design landscape, however, I didn't see many spaces for Black women that allowed them to do this type of radical imagination for themselves, particularly in a loving community.

Toni Morrison famously said, "If there's a book that you want to read, but it hasn't been written yet, then you must write it." I didn't see enough places for Black women to have space to think, play, and dream solutions for themselves and their communities. What I often saw instead were folks outside of our communities given the time and resources to bring in the solutions and ideas they thought were best for us. Taking Toni Morrison's advice, I decided to build the thing I didn't see. Over the last three years I, along with a community of Black women, have cocreated a space of radical imagination and curiosity. Sitting at the intersection of racial healing, mental wellness support, and community design, Colored Girls Liberation Lab (The Lab), is carving out a space for Black women to practice freedom in community. We believe healed, healthy, and whole Black women build healed, healthy, and whole communities. And when given time to rest, think, and imagine, they can come up with wildly creative solutions.

As I offer some of what I've learned on this journey, it's important to share a few definitions and caveats:

1. When I use the term "woman" I am inclusive of all women: cis women, trans women, and nonbinary people who have experiences that align with femininity.
2. The thoughts and experiences shared here are snapshots of a subset of Black women at a particular point in time. These ideas are not exhaustive or representative of every Black woman. What is shared should be seen as inspiration, not as a blueprint.
3. Designing liberated spaces for Black women should be done with Black women, their leadership, and their needs at the center. If you're a Black woman, I hope these ideas serve as validation and inspiration for the types of spaces you deserve to have. If you're not a Black woman, these ideas should be used to open dialogue to create spaces *with* Black women, not *for* them.

Started with a Breast Pump . . . Now We're Here

In 2018, I helped produce the Make the Breast Pump Not Suck Hackathon at the Massachusetts Institute of Technology. This second iteration of the hackathon sought to be more intentional about equity and inclusion, particularly uplifting voices of mothers and birthing people who were most impacted by this issue of the breast pump, well, sucking.

Traditionally, hackathons, which are short design sprints done with a team, are filled with men, usually white men, spending a weekend coming up with their next great idea. Our hackathons sought to use participatory community design to turn the hackathon on its head. Instead of white men being in the room to solve a problem experienced by women and birthing people, the room was filled with women and birthing people designing for themselves. The majority of those folks were Black, Indigenous, and other women of color. Besides the creative innovations made in this space, the mindsets of the participants changed throughout the experience. They began to see themselves as innovators, capable of solving their own community problems when given the opportunity and resources.

Two additional hackathons followed this one, all filled with underestimated and underrepresented identities, solving the problems that were most pressing for them, through a lens of design. I began to wonder what it would look like to create a space where Black women, specifically, could do the same, by using tenets of design, Afrofuturism, and world-building to reimagine their lives and communities.

Welcome to The Lab

When I die, I will not be guilty of having left a generation of girls behind thinking that anyone can tend to their emotional health other than themselves.

—Ntozake Shange

In 2020, Colored Girls Liberation Lab launched as an intergenerational community of support for Black women. The name was inspired by a quote from Ntozake Shange, author of *for colored girls who have considered suicide / when the rainbow is enuf*. In the quote, she talks about ensuring Black girls understand how to tend to their own emotional healing, how to examine it and consider how they hold each other and themselves. Elsewhere, she writes of singing "a black girl's song," a "righteous gospel" that will "let her be born & handled warmly."

Black women deserve places where they can be reborn and held warmly. Colored Girls Liberation Lab felt like the perfect name for a place intended to open up exploration of the possibilities for Black women. As The Lab began to take shape, it was important for me to consider new, radical ways of being in community with Black women. The foundation for The Lab is grounded and influenced by a very intentional set of diverse concepts, literary world-builders, and Black feminist and womanist thinkers:

- *Liberatory and community design frameworks*. These guide our values around collaborative design by those closest to the issue, community accountability, and real-time feedback.
- *Octavia Butler's work, particularly the parables*. Butler fuels the desire to build worlds led by Black women and steeped in radical imagination.
- *Pleasure and the erotic as power as shared by Audre Lorde*. We build spaces that feel good and facilitate pleasure as a way to tap into what we truly desire and open up our imagination.
- *bell hooks's work, particularly Sisters of the Yam*. We use storytelling as a conduit for healing and as an anchor for the way we approach group connection and healing.

The Lab creates and holds space for Black women to heal and reimagine in two ways: through our virtual and in-person gatherings that hold space for healing, exploring, and loving accountability, along with our immersive experiences that allow women to both practice freedom in community and create new paths forward.

Black women deserve places where they can be reborn and held warmly.

Designing Liberated Spaces

In one of my favorite quotes from Robin D. G. Kelley, author of *Freedom Dreams: The Black Radical Imagination*, he says, "Without new visions, we don't know what to build, only what to knock down." We often spend time only considering what isn't working without holding space for completely new visions. Over the last few years, I've asked over two hundred Black women what a liberated future looks like for them. What would the new vision of community look like for us in the future and how do we bring pieces of that future into the present? We've cocreated spaces together and reimagined how support, community, and freedom can look. The design considerations below became our framework for practicing freedom. Through our exploration, six elements emerged for us in the spaces that felt the freest: spaces for healing, dreaming, pleasure, rest, joy, and play.

Some spaces included all of these elements, while others included only one or two, but these elements of freedom, which we began calling our Liberation Bloomprint, summarize what our community needs to both live freely for themselves and reimagine the future for Black communities.

Elements of the Liberation Bloomprint. Image courtesy of Colored Girls Liberation Lab, Inc. Reprinted with permission.

Designing for Healing and Dreaming

Healing takes place within us as we speak the truth of our lives.

—bell hooks, *Sisters of the Yam: Black Women and Self-Recovery*

When the pandemic hit in 2020, many of us had never experienced such long stretches of time without the love and care of community. We were being bombarded with a racial reckoning of sorts, but one that Black folks, particularly Black women, always knew would eventually happen. Watching racial injustice unfold on our television screens without the ability to gather left many of us in pain and unable to see a way forward. Asking anyone to dream of something new felt almost laughable during that summer, particularly for Black women. The times we were in illuminated the need to first have spaces to heal, spaces to tell the truth of our lives and be validated before dreaming of something new.

In her book *Sisters of the Yam*, bell hooks talks about her group of the same name, where women came to share the stories and truths of their lives. In these spaces women realized they weren't alone in their experiences, that they could practice being tender, being lovingly supportive, and conspiring with each other to solve problems. Inspired by this, Dreams & Schemes was launched as a weekly virtual Lab meetup for Black women in late 2020. Each week women join virtually to share their truths centered around our theme for the month. Women explore the futures they want for themselves and also the obstacles holding them back from that future. There are tears, laughs, joys, and triumphs, along with feelings of empowerment and restoration weekly.

Over time, as women have healed through their storytelling, their ability to dream beyond what usually felt possible has expanded. As a result, some women in our community have left jobs or started new ventures to solve community problems. Other women have reimagined the way they do their work, how they incorporate ease and rest into their lives, and how they want to share and create similar experiences with their families.

One of our members said, "I love that everything that I spoke about in Dreams & Schemes in 2022 came to fruition. I appreciate that the space is an incubator for hope, change, and prosperity. A safe habitat for my dreams to grow."

After three years this continues to be The Lab's most transformational space because the power of storytelling in community brings necessary healing when vulnerability, trust, and shared experiences are present. We often hear the phrase "you can't be it if you can't see it." I believe you can't be it if you don't dream it. Often, we need to hear and see the radical imagination in our community for it to be sparked

in ourselves. The sisterhood created in Dreams & Schemes has accelerated the healing journey and made dreaming more possible. Storytelling, healing, and dreaming are connected.

When designing liberatory spaces, consider how you'll create an environment conducive to vulnerability. How can you use storytelling to open a pathway to both healing and radical imagination?

***Generations of Liberation*, illustration by Arrian Maize. Reprinted with permission.**

Designing for Pleasure

For the erotic is not a question of what we do; it is a question of how acutely and fully we can feel in the doing. Once we know the extent to which we are capable of feeling that sense of satisfaction and completion, we can then observe which of our various life endeavors bring us closest to that fullness.

—Audre Lorde, *Uses of the Erotic: The Erotic as Power*

"I don't remember the last time I thought about what made me feel good." This statement from one of our members last year illuminated why creating intentional spaces for pleasure is a necessary practice for liberation. As Audre Lorde writes in *Uses of the Erotic: The Erotic as Power*, pleasure (the erotic) creates an understanding of our deepest desires. Once we know what we truly desire, it makes it easier to seek out anything that aligns with that feeling. Black women are not often given time to figure out what they desire. For many of us, being the first in our families to attend college or to get the job that indicates success can make us feel as if our path has already been laid out for us.

Designing opportunities for women in The Lab to experience, discuss, and reimagine pleasure in various forms has opened up their ability to better choose what aligns with their reimagined life. They are able to question whether the choices they have been making have been for themselves or aligned to a predetermined plan of what it means to be successful in our society.

When designing spaces for pleasure, consider ways to help expand the definition of pleasure through experience and discussion. How do folks experience pleasure through all their senses? How can pleasure direct them to better understand when to say yes and when to say no?

Once we know what we truly desire, it makes it easier to seek out anything that aligns with that feeling.

Designing for Rest

I dream of a day when Black women exist in this world as cared for. When they can operate in the fullness of their magic because they aren't distracted by the work, care, and responsibility for others.

—Colored Girls Liberation Lab Member

Our society, built on capitalism and patriarchy, glorifies the grind. Black women in particular often grind away in their jobs and careers, while also carrying the majority of the physical and mental load in their homes. If you're a woman who is successful in your career, you've likely been rewarded for lack of rest and promoted for devoting most of your time to your profession or business. But grind culture has gotten us nowhere. If we want to design liberated spaces for Black women, creating space for radical rest in various forms is necessary.

Whether actual physical naps, creative rest through art or movement, daydreaming sessions, or retreats, Black women need space to practice turning off their thinking and resting. Many of our Lab immersive experiences are built on a foundation of providing time for rest and reflection on rest. These reflections usually bring up questions about what our society deems successful. Reimagining rest as a necessary part of our freedom journey allows us to evaluate where and how we spend our time and from where we received those messages. For example, after spending time reflecting on rest, one member mentioned feeling rested only on the weekends. It made her reevaluate how she was spending her time during the week and whether her current profession was aligned with the life of ease she was dreaming about.

When designing liberated spaces for rest, consider how to provide varying forms of rest for practice. If you lead a group or organization, how can you plan for moments of rest throughout various projects? If you're in community with Black women, how can you help relieve the invisible burden Black women often feel?

Designing for Joy and Play

Life is a lab. We use this as a mantra in our space to remind us that life has been created for us to play, have fun, and figure it out. White men, in particular, are often encouraged to play. They are given time to "fail up" and try various spaces or opportunities to see what fits. Black women deserve the space to do this as well, but we often can't take the risks to play and change our minds. I believe one of the most transformative elements of The Lab is when Black women come to the realization of

this "life is a lab" mantra. Creating the space for joy and fun and play helps remove the need for perfectionism and affords the opportunity to just try things out for size.

One of our members said, "I think what I love about The Lab so much is the fact that it removes the need to be right or perfect. We're playing and building on experiences while building community." Both joy and play are acts of resistance in a world where Black folks, and especially Black women, are told there is no reason to be joyful or playful.

When designing spaces of liberation, consider how joy and rest can be used as a form of release. How can you practice play? What types of situations will allow for joy to be created and grow?

Taking It Forward

Along with the practices mentioned here, community and ritual create a solid foundation for the practices in The Lab. None of these practices are as effective alone as they are in community. For us, rituals are the ways we recenter ourselves in our freedom practices. They don't have to be long or complicated, just personalized and consistent. Designing freedom-aligned rituals in loving community helps keep these practices of healing, dreaming, pleasure, rest, joy, and play in constant rotation. The loving accountability from the sisterhood makes the experimentation with our dreams enjoyable and attainable.

When Black women have opportunities to be in spaces that are in stark contrast to the oppressive, capitalistic, patriarchal society we otherwise exist in, creative ideas and connections can naturally emerge from a place of abundance rather than scarcity. The spaces we're cocreating through The Lab allow women to reimagine their own lives and the role they play in social change through a lens of radical imagination.

Black women deserve spaces, of their own design, to practice freedom, to rest, and to dream about our future in community. In the Combahee River Collective Statement, the authors share that the liberation of Black women in turn impacts the liberation of all people; the intersections of our identities would necessitate it. I believe our liberation lies in our ability to have space to radically reimagine our futures. When we make room for Black women to dream, we create the conditions for a radically different future for us all.

Rituals are the ways we recenter ourselves in our freedom practices.

Speakers Kayla Elliott, Kristen Southerland, Ashli Wilson Herbert, Janai Marshall, and Tomeka Carroll at the August 2024 Glory Days storytelling event, where Lab members shared stories of liberation and celebration. Photo courtesy of Jaida Moore, Fiercely Feminine Studios.

Care Better

Making Arts and Humanities Software for Actual Humans

Erik Loyer

Erik Loyer (he/him) makes digital artworks and creative tools that fuse comics and video games with musical performance. He founded the interactive media studio Opertoon in 2008, releasing three narrative-driven titles that have garnered critical acclaim and over half a million downloads. Through Opertoon, Erik originated a pair of digital comics and media composition tools that have been used in classrooms, workshops, and commercial releases. He has designed and developed over a dozen interactive nonfiction works in collaboration with leading scholars, artists, and organizations, including the Martin Luther King, Jr. Research and Education Institute. Erik's work has been exhibited in the Americas and Europe, and he has been commissioned by the Whitney Museum of American Art, the Museum of Contemporary Art, Los Angeles, and the San Francisco Museum of Modern Art. He is currently a creative technologist at the regenerative design studio Spherical, crafting interactive media to support the renewal of Los Angeles County's water infrastructure.

Software design at its best embodies an ethos of care: attention paid, in digital form, to the real needs of other human beings. Yet care is neither simple nor easy; it occurs in many forms, across many domains. Care is messy: We can simultaneously care in important, necessary ways, while causing harm in other, neglected ones. Sometimes care for the self expands into care for others, without us realizing it; and sometimes the nature of the care we express in the present makes that same care inaccessible to people in the future. What remains the same is the opportunity we're faced with—to care better, more thoroughly, more justly, now.

Anxiety about uncaring software has been with us as long as software has existed (and perhaps earlier if you include science fiction), but for most of us, those fears took time to become concrete. When software was a novelty, care was an afterthought, and harms were harder to see. Now we're living in a world run by software, and by extension, the problematic worldviews of its makers. Interface is an outgrowth of ideology, and if we're making software of our own, especially software that impacts civic welfare, care is best woven in from the start.

My first attempts at creative coding were really a form of self-care, a way to reassure myself that a nerdy, anxious, awkward, Black and white boy from the suburbs of Northern California, with limited capitalist ambition, could contribute to the public conversation about digital art. I exploded a poem I had written into a whirl of symbols and digital collage, in the hope that deconstructing each word into photos, videos, and graphic marks would somehow validate my inner landscape, making me more "real" to people I struggled to communicate with in person.

The project did bring me some attention: invitations, exhibitions. But when I asked a group of trusted colleagues for some honest critique, one statement stuck with me: "These symbols you're working with; they're meaningful, but they aren't universal." I had fallen into the classic trap of digital: mistaking transcription for translation. I thought that simply re-creating the things I saw in my head in software—the digital version of "build it and they will come"—was enough. That moment of critique helped me to figure out that for my work to connect with others, it needed to translate the connections that seemed so clear to me in my own head

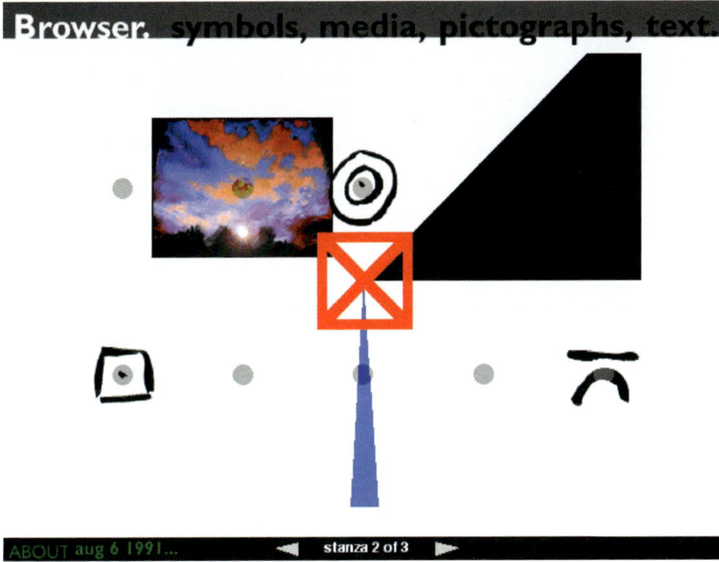

aug 6 1991 (1996, Erik Loyer). Exploding a poem into symbols and digital collage.

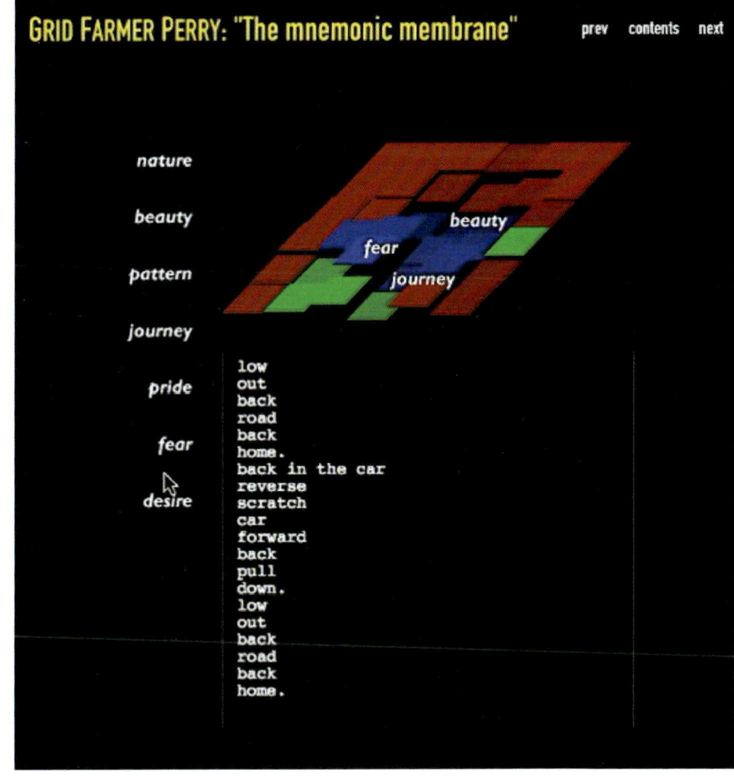

"The mnemonic membrane," from The Lair of the Marrow Monkey (1998, Erik Loyer). Finding ways for users to feel agency within a poem they didn't write.

into a form that could be understood, and acted upon, by real people in the world. It needed to offer them care.

It took another few years before I began to understand how to pull this off. Caught in a wave of layoffs at a brainy video game start-up and thrilled by the radical openness of the early World Wide Web, I returned to my poem. This time, instead of trying to get people to understand it the way I did, I scrambled the words, tossed them into buckets by theme, and then asked users to play with the themes. Each theme could be picked up and dropped over a flexible membrane, causing it to vibrate and emit related excerpts of the poem ("fear" would make it tremble, while "journey" made it flow), accompanied by existential chords.

This approach was a hit with users and introduced me to the world of what would become known as "net art" in a tidy flurry of recognition, exhibitions, and my first travel abroad. At this point the commercial web was only a few years old and still finding its footing; funky experiments and general weirdness abounded (an ad agency even considered adapting the piece for a beer client). Through it all, I was keenly aware that in this new form, the original poem I had written had been almost completely obliterated, along with my hope to place users "inside" it. What took its place was play—joyful explorations directed by users themselves, within the structure I had arranged. I realized that while software-as-art could simply be a vehicle for manifesting the inner landscapes of creators, in order for users to truly feel cared for, they needed to become activators of space, not just tourists in space.

The following years brought opportunities to practice these principles at a new, experimental online academic journal called *Vectors*. *Vectors* was founded by media scholars Tara McPherson and Steve Anderson as a way to explore what scholarly writing could become if it fully engaged the possibilities of digital media—images, sound, video, and interactivity. Grounded in a feminist ethos embracing both theory and practice, the journal brought a team of interactive designers and developers (myself, Raegan Kelly, and Craig Dietrich) together with leading humanities scholars, many of whom were also activists. Our mission? To create "born digital" scholarship that simply couldn't exist in print. A few examples of designs we created for the journal:

- A "test" in which the user, surveilled, must trace shorthand characters in order to "clock in" to an archive of (often highly gendered) materials mandating office efficiency, in Stolen Time Archive (Alice Gambrell and Raegan Kelly)
- Floating words that decompose into poetic critiques of neoliberalism when dunked into the floodwaters of Hurricane Katrina, in Blue Velvet (David Theo Goldberg and Erik Loyer)

- A polyvocal video theater addressing the new visualities of the Iraq War, in Killer Entertainments (Jennifer Terry and Raegan Kelly)
- Monochromatic grids populated with the words of incarcerated women, in Public Secrets (Sharon Daniel and Erik Loyer)
- A glitchy deconstruction of the military and colonial underpinnings of aerial photography, in Dead Reckoning (Caren Kaplan and Raegan Kelly)
- Interactive threads that, when pulled and tangled, reveal feminist perspectives on Persian carpet making, in Nation on the Move (Minoo Moallem and Erik Loyer)

Each of these projects required care on multiple levels—the first of which was care for the scholars we worked with. By bringing peer-reviewed humanities research into such close proximity with interaction design, we were attempting to demonstrate new models for scholarly production, but as a result, the making of *Vectors* could be an intense experience. Some scholars encountered a "crisis moment" where the strange codes and atomizing practices of digital design would provoke so much stress that a way forward seemed impossible. At those moments, designers and editors had to find ways to let the scholars know both that their concerns were valid and also that their work was in good hands.

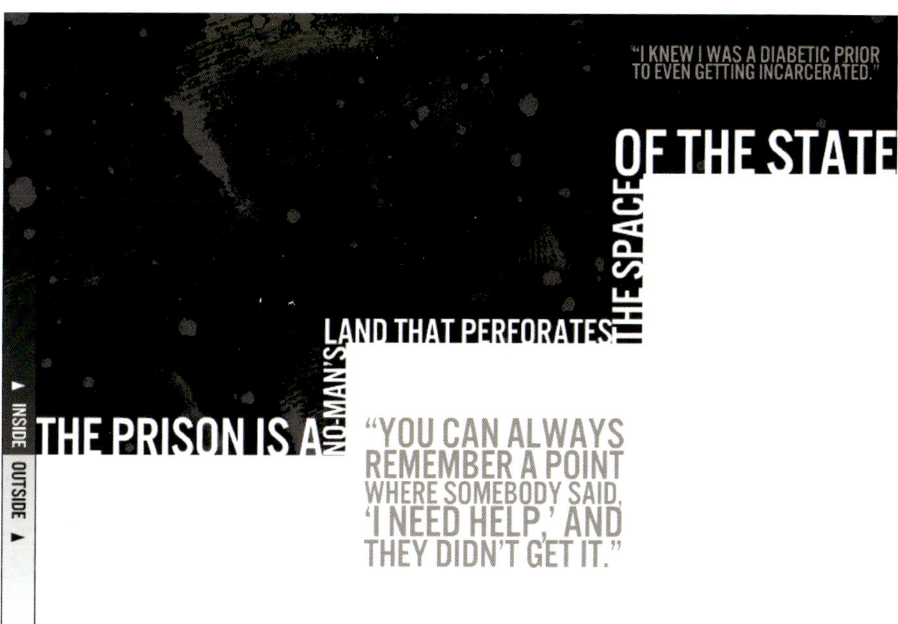

Public Secrets (2007, Sharon Daniel and Erik Loyer). Sharing the testimonies of women incarcerated in California.

Killer Entertainments (2007, Jennifer Terry and Raegan Kelly). A polyvocal video theater addressing the new visualities of the war in Iraq.

Likewise, scholars needed to be generous with us, the people who were interpreting their research in new ways that likely seemed jarring or discordant at times. Each party's care and willingness to speak frankly to the other, often motivated by a mutual desire to see the project have an impact in the world, became key to creating an environment where good work was possible. In the journal *Design Studies* (November 2011), designer Anne Burdick and media critic Holly Willis described the *Vectors* flow this way: "Project teams develop a *shared vocabulary, working process, and cross-disciplinary respect and understanding* which are manifest in innovative projects" (emphasis mine). For a much deeper dive into the origins and outcomes of *Vectors*, see Tara McPherson's book, *Feminist in a Software Lab: Difference + Design*.

Of course, care also needed to be extended to the users of these projects—and there were internal debates about exactly what that meant. Apple's design ethos of glossy digital seamlessness was ascendant at the time, and I was fully on board with it, always in search of the highest frame rates and smoothest motion I could muster; others on the team who were more versed in media theory than I encouraged the troubling of that apparent ease with interfaces that emphasized glitches,

discontinuity, and the subversion of expectations. Over the life of the journal I came to appreciate the strengths and weaknesses of both approaches. When does care mean not giving users what they expect, and in what registers? Can frustration be a form of care? (Honestly, I'm still all about high frame rates, but know thyself, right?)

Many of these positive dynamics were at least partially enabled by our choice to work with the closed, proprietary technology Flash, which made possible the kinds of rich interactivity we wanted to create. The majority of *Vectors* projects were produced in Flash, a choice that would come back to haunt us in exactly the ways predicted by our critics—low accessibility, followed by obsolescence. On December 31, 2020, fifteen years after the launch of *Vectors*, Flash reached the end of its life, instantly breaking the lion's share of works in the journal, along with thousands of games, art projects, and experiments across the internet. As of this writing, Adobe has, for legal reasons, refused to release the source code for Flash, and independent attempts to preserve Flash works have been only partially successful.

Was this a failure of care? If the *Vectors* team could go back to the mid-2000s, knowing what we know now about the fate of the journal, would we make different choices? Speaking for myself, I'd like to believe that I would put greater effort into providing accessible alternatives to the rich Flash-based interfaces we were creating. What appeared to be a stark binary at the time, with innovation on the one side and openness on the other, likely held subtler opportunities. In the end, however, I'd still create those rich interfaces, short-lived though they were. In *Vectors* we had a singular chance to show care in the flawed ways we were able to, in the moment we were given—and I'm glad that we took it.

As an aside, while Flash is gone, it's important to note that choices between open and proprietary technologies remain, and will likely always be with us. Today these discussions are happening around social media networks, mobile apps, game engines, and augmented and virtual reality. If you're a creator wanting to learn more about how to approach these choices with accessibility and longevity in mind, I highly recommend a read of *Acid-Free Bits*, a digital publication from the Electronic Literature Organization, on exactly this topic.

As *Vectors* progressed, it became clear that the kind of care we exercised as editors and designers of bespoke interactive essays was too costly to be sustainable. As a result, near the end of the 2000s, members of *Vectors'* core team began exploring the idea of a new piece of software—a publishing tool for scholars creating long-form, rich media essays—that would be free and open-source. This new tool would resemble blogging software much more than the intricate art house creations *Vectors* published. The lush designs we delivered using proprietary technologies

Care, in software as much as in anything else, is what sets the table for people to act in ways most likely to bring about collective benefit.

now needed to be replaced with standards-based approaches and infused with different forms of care. I'll admit to a bit of prideful skepticism of the approach. Surely, our painstaking work couldn't be turned into templates that could be deployed in our absence?

Nevertheless, we launched ourselves into the task at hand. It quickly became clear that this new software, which we named Scalar as an obscure joke (in mathematics, a "scalar" is a value that multiplies vector quantities, just as we hoped Scalar would multiply the influence of *Vectors*), was a tool for scaffolding digital humanities publications. Building on the legacies of hypertext, and anticipating future knowledge management tools like Notion, Scalar took the structural building blocks of online publishing—the linear sequencing of blogs, the nonlinear indexing of tags, and the strengths of annotated media—and allowed users to mix them in a wide variety of combinations, in ways that seemed to be a good fit for humanities scholars.

While daunting to design, ultimately this openness and flexibility in structure would motivate tens of thousands of users around the world to create a dizzying array of projects, many directly engaged with issues of social justice and liberation, for ten years and counting—a powerful reminder that care, in software as much as in anything else, is what sets the table for people to act in ways most likely to bring about collective benefit. These projects include the following:

- A critical edition of poetry, drama, and fiction written by Black women during the Harlem Renaissance, in "Women of the Early Harlem Renaissance: African American Women Writers 1900–1922" (Amardeep Singh)
- A video collection of the oral teachings of the Indigenous elder Elsie Paul, in As I Remember It: Teachings (ʔəms taʔaw) from the Life of a Sliammon Elder (Elsie Paul, Davis McKenzie, Paige Raibmon, and Harmony Johnson)
- A digital exhibit documenting the harmful outcomes of misguided science and pseudoscience in women's mental healthcare, in *A Case of Hysteria* (Anne-Marie Maxwell, Tyson Gaskill)
- A science fiction story about the experiences of a trans woman of color and climate refugee, in "Redshift & Portalmetal" (micha cárdenas)
- A year-long blog guiding readers through an archive of digitized Black newspapers from the twentieth century, in *Black Quotidian* (Matthew F. Delmont)

Black Quotidian **(2019, Matthew F. Delmont). Exploring an archive of twentieth-century Black newspapers, one day at a time.**

Scholars using Scalar's free and familiar blog-like interface could assemble and publish their projects in a highly readable online format, and for most of our users, that was enough. One of the hidden strengths of Scalar, however, is its API, or "application programming interface." An API is a way for a piece of software to make its features available to other software. This meant that for those projects that had additional support, bespoke interfaces could be created using the API to gather that content and then present it in a completely unique way. A standards-based foundation for as rich a digital experience as we could dream up, this, finally, was a sustainable fusion of the approaches that were so difficult to merge when we were making *Vectors*.

One example was a project called Freedom's Ring, commissioned by the Martin Luther King, Jr. Research and Education Institute at Stanford, for the fiftieth anniversary of the "I Have a Dream" speech. In this project, artist and activist Evan Bissell created an animated digital mural to accompany the recorded speech, annotating it with imagery and a curriculum. Bissell's striking art and thoughtful curation places King's words in both historical and contemporary contexts that help to shake off their accumulated familiarity. I provided design and engineering for the project, which offered the unique and unforgettable pleasure of linking a rich

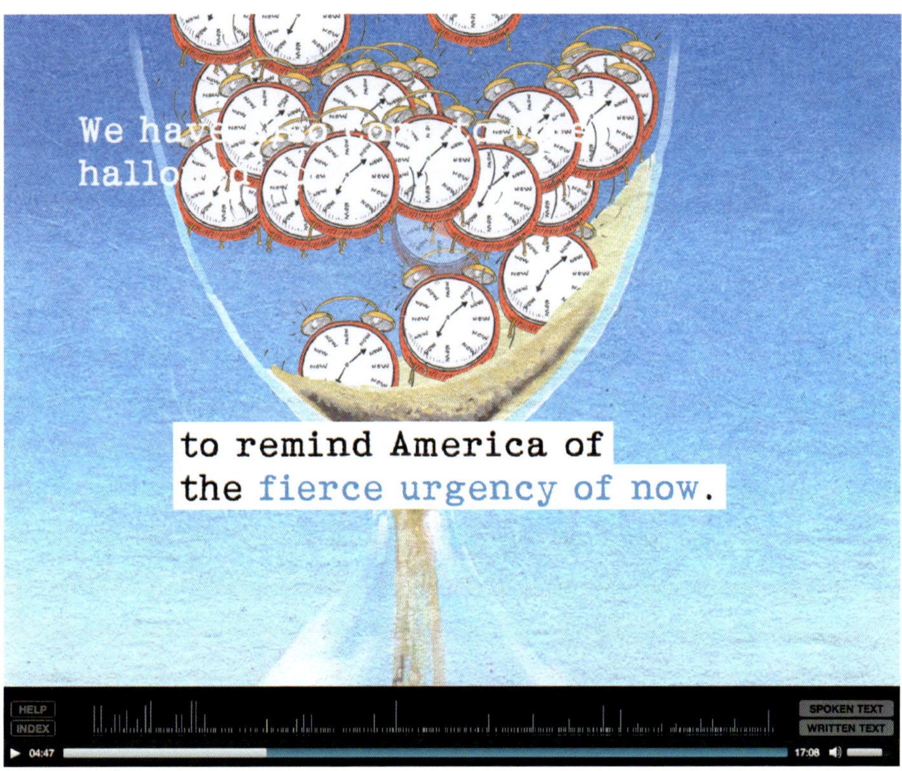

Freedom's Ring (2013, Evan Bissell). An animated, annotated edition of Martin Luther King Jr.'s "I Have a Dream" speech.

collection of animations and annotations to the precise cadences of King's speech. For me, this care was also joy—and Freedom's Ring continues to be shared today, ten years after its original launch.

If digital making has taught me anything, it's that care, for both individuals and communities, is the main source of authentic value in software. Ironically, it's something I still sometimes have to make a conscious effort to remember, because the digital medium makes it easy to fool myself when it comes to caring. I find that I'm still sometimes seduced by the computer's ability to make physical the thoughts orbiting in my head. It seems that somehow the same qualities that make pixels on a screen appear to have weight, to be actual instead of virtual, also make it possible for software to appear caring in some ways, while missing the mark in others.

So much has been made of the accelerating function of digital technology. Software developers feel that acceleration every day, as they search the open web for solutions to the bug they just ran into or for the patterns most useful in tackling their next challenge. Sophisticated applications can be built more quickly than ever before, and artificial intelligence promises to multiply those effects. And yet,

We care imperfectly, but perfection isn't required.

care cannot be accelerated—at least not the kind of care that involves listening at least as much as speaking, that remains open to the possibility that one's operating paradigm contains damaging flaws, and that makes careful, collective judgments about how to remedy and prevent harm. There is no way to care "fast," but external pressures will always tempt us to try.

Most of the negative societal impacts of software amount to largely predictable failures of care. It's true that sometimes software creates entirely new kinds of harm we couldn't have anticipated, but much more often, we simply choose to ignore the harm waiting in the wings because of some other short-term benefit. Often we act in bad faith, and even when we don't, we never get it entirely right. We care imperfectly, but perfection isn't required; just the willingness to look and listen, as early and as often as we can manage, to the people a given design is likely to affect—even to design together with them if we can. Limitations of time, resources, and imagination will always press us to decide, both individually and collectively, where to draw the lines of care. Let's do everything possible to make the circle as wide as we can.

United in Flow

Accessible Pleasure, Game Design, and How We Heal

Latoya Peterson

Latoya Peterson (she/her) lives at the intersection of emerging technology and culture. Named one of *Forbes Magazine*'s 30 Under 30 Rising Stars in Media, she is best known for the award-winning blog *Racialicious*—the intersection of race and pop culture. She is currently an expert narrative designer at Elsewhere Entertainment, an Activision studio working on a new IP. Previously, she was a cofounder and chief experience officer at Glow Up Games, an award-winning game studio that created a tie-in game for HBO's *Insecure* and a play-and-watch experience for the Oregon Shakespeare Festival called *Hella Iambic*. Known for bringing a hip-hop, feminist, and racial justice framework to technological and cultural analysis, Latoya's perspectives have been widely published in outlets like *Wired*, *Teen Vogue*, NPR, *ESPN the Magazine*, *The New York Times*, *The Washington Post*, *Essence*, *Spin*, *Vibe*, *Marie Claire*, Kotaku, *The Atlantic*, *The American Prospect*, and *The Guardian*.

Part 1: Play

> I be in a flow state, flow state
> Everything is okay, okay
> I be in a flow state, flow state
> Everything is okay, okay
>
> I'm just going with the flow, catching all the waves.
>
> **—"Flow State," Londrelle**

As long as I can remember, I've dealt with situations in my life in three specific ways: I read my way through it, I write my way through it, or I play my way through it. Every time I feel myself tumbling down the cliffs of life, my lifelines are always books, pen and paper, or a controller firmly in my hands.

Gaming has allowed me to access deep parts of myself through the soothing state of flow. When I had my first adult breakup, I comforted myself with Tidus and Yuna's journey to defeat Sin and save Spira in *Final Fantasy X*. After a close friend's suicide during the pandemic, I would pour myself a drink in real life and spend some time basking in the vibes at the jazz bar in Kichijoji in *Persona 5: The Royal*. After my miscarriage, I spent hours hoeing fields and sowing seeds in *Stardew Valley*. And after my father died, I took my son with me into *Spiritfarer*, sailing around in our little boat, cooking food, and gently guiding spirits to the afterlife.

But why is the practice of play so soothing?

The answer can be found in the idea of a *flow state*: the feeling of total immersion in a task or activity. Flow state isn't exclusively achieved through gaming. Many other activities can also allow for flow, everything from woodworking to dance to martial arts.

In his 2017 GDC talk "Designing a Trance: Meditation and Game Design,"[1] game and sound designer Robin Arnott explored the magic of a flow state, likening it to a controllable trance. After exploring consciousness hacking, neuroscience,

meditation, and prayer, he developed a framework to pull those same types of mental states and apply them to games.

The initial answer seems simple: games create a playable loop and intrinsic reward for your actions. The simulation aspect also removes all the real-life barriers of something like gardening—bugs, finicky soil, hot weather—and condenses the experience into a three-dimensional meditative experience.

Gaming in many ways is controlled frustration—as opposed to real life, which is *uncontrolled* frustration. The games we play are a choice: We made a conscious decision in downloading or purchasing something to play, and we are rewarded with different options of escape.

But the magic is in the doing. Games provide consistent feedback through a gameplay loop that is designed to feel like a measurable accomplishment. And that's really important when life starts feeling sticky after a massive traumatic incident. One of the horrible things about trauma is that we end up in many ways trapped inside of that moment. Many people who experience trauma also experience deep depression and grief, and may feel stuck processing their experience in a trance-like state.

Let's return to Robin Arnott's presentation. To define a trance, he uses Dennis Wier's definition from *The Way of Trance*,[2] simply stating that a trance is a self-perpetuating mental loop. But there are also other ways that we experience a self-perpetuating mental loop. Do you ever find yourself obsessively revisiting a situation over and over again?

In *Everyday Trauma*, author Tracey Shors looks at the pattern of rumination that tends to occur after a traumatic event. Rumination, she writes, is when thoughts "cycle through the brain over and over again." Different from worries, which are often focused on problem solving, Shors explains that "ruminations are autobiographical and directed at oneself" and rarely create positive outcomes for the ruminator. Instead, Shors concludes, "Ruminating keeps our attention on ourselves and weakens our ability to pay attention" to the present.[3]

It can be easy to find our brains stuck in a negative or unhealthy pattern, especially after a period of setbacks. But one of the core tenets of game design is helping players navigate a set of obstacles. If players are failing in one area or part of play, game designers tend to adjust the system to create an environment where more players can be successful. The state of feeling stuck in a game environment is a tricky thing for designers to navigate—while some level of controlled frustration is normal, too much frustration and the players will start abandoning the game.

That was true for me navigating life post–complex trauma—at some point, the amount of grief took its toll and started graying out my world. Experts term this "anhedonia,"[4] a symptom of depression where nothing feels fun anymore.

Gaming in many ways is controlled frustration.

Most days I felt too mentally exhausted to meaningfully contribute to real life. That stuck feeling persisted during most activities—except when I wound down for the day with one of my favorite games, *Spiritfarer*. Instead of forcing my way through the challenges of day-to-day living, I found respite in a comforting and cozy game world with clear, relaxing tasks and achievable goals.

The core objective of *Spiritfarer* is to manage the afterlife and eventual death transition of the different spirits who come to live on your houseboat. After completing various quests for each spirit, you unlock more of their backstories until they ask to go to the Everdoor, a gateway from which they will not return. This description may seem intense, but the playable loop is simple and calming. As Stella (an updated version of the boatman on the river Styx), you and your cat spend your days fishing, building the ship, tending to your garden, crafting materials, making meals, catching stars, and listening to the needs and stories of the various people on the ship.

The repetition is soothing, lulling the player into a flow state. Pull weeds, make food, talk to spirits, repeat. Unlike the unhelpful repetition that happens during rumination, the soothing repetition of small, achievable tasks in games has the opposite effect on the body—it creates a calming sensation.

By focusing on bringing ourselves from an agitated state to a calmer state, we can begin to forge a new pathway and framework for healing after intense periods of events. One of the best ways to soothe an overtaxed brain and body seems counterintuitive during a depressive state but is so vital: doing things that spark pleasure.

Part II: Pleasure

> You can be the light
> Let 'em throw the shade
> Light is here to stay
> Never fade, flow state
>
> Just being in that state of flow
> Being in that place of grace
> Being in that state of nonresistance
> To life, to love
> To whatever way life wants to flow

—"Flow State," Londrelle

If anhedonia (the loss of pleasure) is a direct result of depression and stress, one path to healing could be to specifically focus on increasing activities that bring pleasure or happiness.

But that is easier said than done. Many people experience happiness going outside for a hike, seeing friends, or practicing an instrument, but in times of stress most of us reach for other activities that are less soul-nourishing. Doomscrolling happens for a reason—even as we know we should be doing other things, we end up losing hours to the comforting, endless loop of social media, passively consuming image after image.

While often vilified as another waste of time, gaming provides the brain with a form of intentional pleasure *combined* with an intentional feedback loop. Some would attribute this to intentional hits of dopamine programmed into the design of popular games, but the allure of play has a deeper foundation. Gaming does provide dopamine, but it also provides a sense of accomplishment, community, and joy. In some ways, the core loop in gameplay is a map representing the creation of pleasure in players.

Perhaps we can use the framework of the gameplay loop as we think about remapping the mind toward better outcomes. Just like the small hints from a tutorial aiding players in achieving a goal, we want to nudge our minds away from a recurring negative feedback loop toward loops that feel more positive and rewarding. One activist framework that may hold some interesting possibilities would be to combine the lessons from game design with the politics of pleasure.

Before I dive into pleasure politics, I want to note that this isn't a dressed-up

version of the power of positive thinking. Often, people in crisis are advised to think positively or told that their thoughts control their outcomes, which is cold comfort to a person facing housing instability or food insecurity. While this advice is given with the best intentions, a person who is tormented by their own thoughts or the words and actions of others may not be able to simply shift their brain into a more positive space.

Such thinking can be harmful as it requires us to mask what is happening for fear of judgment—something many people dealing with depression or complex grief have already experienced. In *Supersurvivors*, authors David B. Feldman and Lee Daniel Kravetz dismiss the idea of toxic positivity in favor of something much better: the idea of grounded hope. After our sense of reality changes, the authors advocate applying a simple formula: "a realistic view of the situation + a strong view of one's ability to control one's destiny through one's efforts = grounded hope."[5]

For the purposes of this piece, the word "remapping" is used intentionally: Our brains love to seek familiar patterns,[6] and so established patterns tend to be reinforced, even if the pattern is harmful or self-hating. In order to shift out of the pain, one tactic we can explore is trying to intentionally lay a foundation of pleasure.

Game developer and scholar Jane McGonigal wrote her first book, *Reality Is Broken*,[7] about the many ways in which games make us better—from lucid dreaming to social connection. A few years after publication, McGonigal had a traumatic brain injury that forced her to relearn everything. Out of this experience, she published a game and book called *SuperBetter*,[8] deeply exploring how games can help brains and bodies heal.[9]

But I want to push this idea a little further: If a key component of depression is anhedonia, then rewiring the brain toward pleasure becomes a matter of necessity and I would argue an integral part of the healing practice.

From a healing perspective, we can learn a lot from pleasure activists. adrienne maree brown, who literally wrote the book on pleasure activism, gives a succinct definition of the politics of pleasure in an interview with the ACLU:

> The nutshell of pleasure activism is really, how do we make justice and liberation the most pleasurable activities we can engage in and how do we imbue the pleasurable things that we do in our lives with justice and liberation. And a lot of it is about reclaiming our right to feel pleasure. For those of us who have experienced oppression, those of us who are living inside of systems that are structured around us, denying what we feel and just participating in the system and making it go and making it work. There's a lot of

> healing involved in pleasure activism like learning to feel satisfied and content in your life as it is right now.[10]

But why is pleasure an imperative on this healing journey?

For one, pleasure tends to be stigmatized, especially in conversations about healing. The goal is to feel better and to feel good, but practices like talk therapy and self-help tend to feel like work. Pleasure tends to be put into a box, away from the "serious work" of healing. However, finding pleasure in day-to-day life is essential to the process of recovery.

Audre Lorde, feminist mother, pioneered the modern concept of self-care in her essay "A Burst of Light," where she writes in an epilogue to her journal entries, "Caring for myself is not self-indulgence, it is self-preservation and that is an act of political warfare." All throughout her battle with cancer, she seeks solace and refuge in pleasure, from Bob Marley's music to the arms of her lover Frances.

Games are a form of accessible pleasure. At any moment, at any time, using anything from a pencil to the highest-end AR headset, games allow the player to transport out of their current reality into a different world. Even simple games like *Snake* on the iconic Nokia 6110 phone or *Drug Wars* on the TI-83 calculator took players from wherever they may be in the physical world and into a world of their own choosing.

Finding pleasure in day-to-day life is essential to the process of recovery.

Games invite you to rewrite your current narrative by becoming the hero (or antihero in some cases) in an environment where you face challenging, but surmountable, odds. And the end goal is a pleasurable experience—to create a sense of control and satisfaction in a set outcome. During play, I have done everything from rolling up crabs and paperclips to please a cantankerous king of the cosmos in *Katamari Damacy* to throwing toilet paper at a giant ball of poo in *Conker's Bad Fur Day*. Yet, no matter how strange the scenario, those core elements of transcendent play are present and bring pleasure to players. While I do not believe I ever want to lob rolls of toilet paper at a poop monster in real life, the design of the game made that gross action a pleasurable and hilarious activity. When we play, we make the pursuit of pleasure a concrete practice.

Part III: Practice and Playlist

> Setting your intentions
> And allowing those intentions to unfold beautifully
> Magically, abundantly, miraculously
>
> **—"Flow State," Londrelle**

Claiming pleasure from unexpected places is the most healing practice we can adopt when coping with trauma or grief. At the 2024 Worlds in Play conference, I had the privilege of viewing three distinct live art performance pieces dealing with memory, pleasure, and grief.

Artist Robert Karimi presented two experiences—the first, "The Mint Experience,"[11] is an excerpt from one of his longer shows about the persistence of memory. Audience members are asked to regard a simple mint leaf—to examine the look, feel, scent, and taste as Karimi tells a story about his mother soothing him with a cup of mint tea. The second, "Please Open Your Mouth,"[12] is an excerpt from artist Joanna Garner's multihour exploration of food and pleasure. Standing with our eyes closed, we in the audience were asked to deeply surrender to the pleasure of taste, erotically rolling a piece of fruit around our mouths and being vocally coached by Garner ("Lick it! Suck it! Put your tongue in it!"). The experience was designed to highlight the pleasurable potential in a simple bite of food. Karimi's final piece, "My Grief Is a Watermelon," dealt with bittersweet pleasure—when a treasured memory (in this case, his grandfather's love of watermelon-flavored candy) transforms into a different, more melancholy feeling after his grandfather dies.

All three pieces dealt with pleasure, but in very different ways. The first highlighted the role of pleasure and the sensory ways to recall pleasurable memories even years after they occur; the second explored the erotic potential of everyday actions and how that imbues our lives with dozens of accessible pleasures daily; and the final piece, a deep meditation on pain, pleasure, and grief, underscored the need to carry forward the sweetness of life even while dealing with the weight of loss.

After surviving so much for so long, it is vital to remember that there is pleasure in opting back into life. Anhedonia strips the color from life; it is the power of pleasure that allows us to return to our understanding of our full lived experience. What we learn from games is that pleasure can be designed, pleasure can be programmed, and pleasure can come from unexpected sources. If we embrace the idea of pleasure as a *practice*, perhaps we can forge different, more pleasurable paths to healing.

Now, let's turn to how we practice.

In periods of deep transformation, sometimes it is more than enough to keep putting one foot in front of the other. When times are difficult, the act of survival is the only thing that needs to happen—sometimes, the victory is making it to see another day. Just like with physical injury, we will need to spend some time tending to ourselves after emotional injury. One way to achieve this is to become intentional about a healing practice, a way to rebuild ourselves after trying times. While this practice may look different depending on what your personal journey has been, below are some ideas to play with.

First, let's play with intentionally bringing ourselves into a flow state.

Pick a game that you love to play. Make sure it is familiar and something you could spend hours playing. If no games come to mind, you can always download *Tetris*. Or you could play other puzzle-based games: *Candy Crush*, *Two Dots*, and *Wordscapes* are all easy entry and easily accessible on a mobile device.

Or take this opportunity to drop back into a created world you loved. Is it time to rediscover the *Legend of Zelda*? Replay *Crash Bandicoot* or *Spyro*? Buy a new Tamagotchi? Deliver a gravity-defying beatdown in *Tekken*? Whatever you choose, try to remember the feelings of playing. What was your emotional state during and after you played?

Play your game of choice when you have some clear time—hopefully an hour—and just surrender yourself to the game.

After playing, observe your mental state. Do you feel the same, slightly happier, or slightly depressed after playing?

Think (or journal) about the following:

1. What are the signs you notice when you feel stress? When something is painful? How do you normally soothe yourself?
2. By switching that practice to play, did you feel more or less stressed after the hour? If you feel more stressed, why? Is there something more pressing than taking time for yourself in this moment?
3. Did you feel a state of flow while playing? Why or why not? If not, do you believe you were distracted? Or was something else blocking the flow?
4. How can you bring a presence of flow into small, day-to-day activities like chores or commuting?

Practicing accessible states of flow helps to reconnect us to ourselves, to be present when our thoughts want to pull us into the past or the future, to avoid rumination in favor of practices that are self-soothing. The most essential thing to remember is that flow state, just like the power of our breath, is always accessible and always here. All you need is yourself.

Notes

Epigraph: Lyrics on pages 145, 148, and 151 from "Flow State," by Londrelle, 2022. Reprinted with permission.

1 Robin Arnott, "Designing a Trance: Meditation and Game Design," https://www.gdcvault.com/play/1024156/Designing-a-Trance-Meditation-and.

2 Dennis R. Wier, ed., *The Way of Trance* (2007, Trance Research Foundation).

3 Tracy Shors, *Everyday Trauma: Remapping the Brain's Response to Stress, Anxiety, and Painful Memories for a Better Life* (Flatiron Books, 2021), 52.

4 "Anhedonia: A Concept Analysis," National Library of Medicine, accessed July 25, 2023, https://www.ncbi.nlm.nih.gov/pmc/articles/PMC3664836/.

5 David B. Feldman and Lee Daniel Kravetz, *Supersurvivors: The Surprising Link Between Suffering and Success* (Harper, 2014), 43.

6 J. J. Sparkes, "Pattern Recognition and a Model of the Brain," *International Journal of Man-Machine Studies* 1, no. 3, (July 1969): 263–78.

7 Jane McGonigal, *Reality Is Broken: Why Games Make Us Better and How They Can Change the World* (Penguin Press, 2011).

8 SuperBetter, https://superbetter.com/.

9 Jane McGonigal, "Heal Your Brain with Video Games," video, filmed at TED2014, https://www.youtube.com/watch?v=9zyNcov087U.

10 "The Politics of Pleasure," *At Liberty Podcast*, ACLU with adrienne maree brown, March 3, 2022, https://www.aclu.org/podcast/the-politics-of-pleasure.

11 Robert Karimi, "The Mint Experience! UI, Worldbuilder, or How I Learned to Love the Non-Technological Sensorial Gestures That Created Booms of Deliciousness!," session at Worlds in Play, Mesa, AZ, January 7, 2024, https://worldsinplay.com/Robert-Karimi.

12 Joanna Garner, "Please Open Your Mouth," session at Worlds in Play, Mesa, AZ, January 7, 2024, https://worldsinplay.com/Joanna-Garner.

Reflections on Process

Susu Attar

(in conversation with Sangita Shresthova)

Susu Attar (she/her) is a multimedia artist born in Baghdad and raised in Los Angeles, where she lives. Susu's individual and communal practices explore themes including mourning, hospitality, healing, and renewal. Her work across mediums often documents and reimagines struggles for self-determination, from the level of the individual to the family and from local communities to transnational diasporas. Through her wide-ranging approach, Susu examines existing frameworks within both everyday life and political movements and creates new contexts that center the notion of art as a means of transformation and a space of interconnection. Susu's commitment to building narratives that open up future possibilities for both individual and collective agency has led her to extend her practice to production design, curating, creative direction, and world-building. As an educator, she has produced and facilitated programs and workshops in the United States and abroad, utilizing art practices to expand communal imagination. Susu is a member of SEPIA Collective, a women of color art collective whose work includes a traveling exhibition, *ICONIC: Black Panther*.

Origins

I come from very empowering parents, though I wouldn't have said this as a kid. In hindsight, I can see that the toughness and resilience that my dad instilled in me and my brothers prepared us for a challenging world. And the gratitude mindset and spirituality my mother instilled taught me how to pull from ancient wisdom and forces greater than myself.

My family's story is inextricably tied to our Iraqi roots. We are from a country that has been in some sort of war my entire life, and even before I existed. As Americans, we also live within the borders of the country that has waged these wars. It's a very strange position: to be of two places that are constantly at odds. And yet, here I am.

Visual Instinct

Visual communication has always come naturally to me. I've been making images since I was two or three years old. I suppose I could always express more through my hands than I could through words. Even as I grew older and more thoughtful, my ideas would come out as visuals first, and then I would try to find words to describe them. And when the visuals got more complex, I'd ask my oldest brother, Laith, who was an incredible artist: *How do I make this?*

I tend to think you can show more than you can tell. With images, there is more room for feeling our way toward individual understanding instead of intellectualizing and coming to general conclusions. There's a chance to make someone react emotionally before their preprogrammed prejudices limit comprehension of the information being shared.

Languages Collide

Visual language is culturally specific.

Studying art in college made it clear to me that Western languages and worldviews dominate the way art is understood. It seems so obvious now, but at the time, it helped me understand how exactly I was different from the prevailing American

art world culture. I was using visual language rooted in Iraqi and Arab notions of expression and highly influenced by Black American renaissance paintings and Mexican mural traditions. These were the references in my house and community. This is the art that taught me how to make art. In the classroom, my references were considered obscure or otherwise unknown to my classmates, and so they could only interpret my work through their own references. I found their interpretations of colors and symbols to be concrete, not leaving room for diverse understanding.

In my frustration, I realized I had to learn how to translate my visual language into theirs. Otherwise, I would find my work being interpreted according to their ideas, their aesthetics, their definitions. This was a very difficult thing for me even as I navigated subtle and not-so-subtle suggestions of how I should behave and create based on my culture.

I was becoming an artist and had to contend with the same assumptions that I faced everywhere else in my life. It turned out art was not a liberated space. Colonial constructs and biases follow you everywhere in America.

Photographs

Painting abstractly teaches me things. I started to wonder what it could teach me about images—war media.

My work with war media was born out of the second American war in Iraq. The "shock and awe" bombardment campaign was reported through journalists embedded within US allied forces. Media had become blatantly weaponized. I was seeing countless images of the horrific scenes of war raining down on Iraqis in the news every day, images of people running for their lives and being un-alived all from the point of view of the US military. I started thinking on how a photograph—seemingly a document of something real—gives us a sense that we have actually seen something we, in fact, have not. Photography creates a false sense of knowing. It lays claim to being a document of reality, a horrific reality that most of us have not seen for ourselves. It's framed. It's cropped. There is also a caption that tells us exactly what we're looking at. These edits slip past the general consciousness. Photography shapes the beginning and end of what we need to know.

Almost compulsively, I would save the digital images I found—thousands and thousands of them. At some point, I realized they were a type of collection and began to organize the files in order to use them more frequently.

The massive collection gave way to questions about the effects of war media and photography in general. What does it mean to only see people in violated and traumatized positions? What are we fixing about their stories in our imagination?

What do we assume about their condition, their nature, their lived realities? What can we grasp if we look beyond the image? I have been on a journey to dig deeper into these questions for many years.

Painting Activates the Imagination

I started making paintings of war media, but I made them very vague so that people couldn't clearly see where these images were from. There were no identifiable cultural signifiers. I painted them very large so that the viewer's body and the subject's body could interact.

Instead of monumentalizing Iraqis in distress, I would keep the body posture and obscure everything else through the paint. In order to restore some of the desensitization war media has created, the obscure painting asks the viewer to feel through the meaning of the subject's posture, to relate to it through their own body. Without clear details, the viewer isn't able to come to concrete conclusions. They have to decide for themselves what is happening in the image. And there is more room for any two viewers to come to different conclusions. This is an important exercise, facilitated by the paint.

Our imagination has limitless potential if we exercise it. Images of subjugation and the stories that accompany them can cap our imagination. This is dangerous and needs to be resisted. Imagination activates the whole body and elicits a whole-body response. This is where the role of image making becomes critical toward that resistance.

Susu Attar, *Layover: Jeddah after Somalia, Sudan, Ethiopia & Djibouti, 1979* (2018). Acrylic on tracing paper, 11 × 14 inches. Courtesy of the artist.

My own associations with the postures started to change as I worked with them. I realized that the images of Iraqis flailing also share a posture with Iraqis dancing. When crying, the people in the images kind of look like they're singing. Extracting the body posture initially felt like a further act of violence, another layer of decontextualizing. Then that lack of context seemed to free the body in my imagination and let me see another possibility in the stories they hold. By imagining more for the people in these photos, I can imagine more for myself.

The truth is, I come from a really big world, and I am viewed through a very small lens.

Susu Attar, *because you're mine / i put a spell on you* (2018). Acrylic, coffee, and coffee grounds on paper, 11 × 14 inches. Courtesy of the artist.

Family, Photography

I have always been fascinated by family photos. When I was small, I would go over to people's houses to hang out and I'd ask to look at their family photos. Often, I'd ask to take one of them and my friends would oblige—although their parents probably never knew! I never understood why I had this deep love. It probably has something to do with my father's love for photo making. He was a talented photographer who would document nature and family. To this day, my collection includes photos of friends' families as well as school dance photos and holiday photos. I also have my own family's photo collection, including my father's slide negatives. These are largely of family in Baghdad or family friends in Los Angeles photographing themselves to keep for private collections. I am especially drawn to those photos of in-between moments. The kind where someone looks away, someone is in the middle of their sentence, someone is cropped or blurred. These feel like real-life moments. As real as a still, cropped image can be.

Family photos are specific yet endearing for many. They have been a way for me to bring some humanity back into the conversation and visually expand the space for imagination—for myself and anyone who identifies with the images. As it turns out, my collections are connected. In one collection are photos Iraqis made of themselves. In the other, Iraqis are photographed in the context of war. One is the first-person point of view, and one is the subject as *other*.

Speculative Civic Media

My fascination with photographs is speculative. It's magical nonfiction.

A speculative story can use a real-world concept as a point of departure. My work with photographs invites fictionalized possibilities that are rooted in some reality. Photographs might be limited in perspective or cropped; some reality is acknowledged as the basis for the image.

This is a magical aspect of art—it can invite us to revisit our assumptions. It's a generous invitation in my opinion. With artistic gestures, meanings can change. There is more gray area than black-and-white fixed ideas. It's a small gesture, but it's important. We need our imaginations in order to change the realities in the world. Without expansive vision, there is only the status quo. This applies on individual and collective levels.

Outward Mobility

Regenerative Horizontal Moves in the Face of Confinement

Quetzal Flores

Quetzal Flores (he/him) is a Chican@ musician, producer, and cultural strategist/organizer raised in East Los Angeles. He is the founder and musical director of the Grammy Award–winning Chican@ band Quetzal. From 2012 to 2024 Quetzal served as a program manager for the Alliance for California Traditional Arts, designing and implementing culturally sustainable health equity work in Boyle Heights as well as in prisons across the state. As a producer, Quetzal has contributed to more than one hundred recordings with various artists. Currently, Quetzal is the cofounder and director of cultural justice for the Community Power Collective.

"What do you want it to sound like?" I asked. Alex replied, "We want it to sound like an oldie." I picked up my twelve-string guitar and instantly felt the information igniting in my cellular memory. The ancestral knowledge subversively carried across time and space by guardians of tradition and hope for multiple generations so that I might be able, in a split second, to respond to this moment.

My hands moved . . . C, A minor, F minor, G7. I plucked and strummed through a few cycles, looked up for any affirmation and saw watery eyes, smiles, surrendering, heads bobbing to the rhythm. Fleeting yet transformative moments of connection and vulnerability were a regular occurrence in this space.

We continued to go through the process of creating this song together (a process I call collective songwriting). "Where are we with the lyrics?" I asked. "First came the fear, then came the tears," exclaimed Alex. This song was about what it felt like the moment they realized they were going to be locked up for life or, at best, a very long time. For the next hour we dove into a deep debate on whether in fact the fear, or tears, came first. "Nah man, I felt a lot of fear at first for letting my family down and hurting my wife, kids, and my mom. Then the tears came," shared Jesse. Dowdy chimed in, "For me, it was the opposite. The tears came automatically and then the fear settled in when I really got to thinking about it." Before we knew it our three-hour session was over and Alex said, "Damn, I forgot I was in prison."

Between 2014 and 2016, I doubled as a program manager and teaching artist for the Alliance for California Traditional Arts prison programming. My first assignment was at Corcoran State Prison, which was notorious for various forms of torture and abuse that led to a federal indictment in 1998. On day one, a watch command correctional officer proceeded to scold us, stating, "Why are you teaching here? These guys are criminals! They're animals. They don't deserve anything. Go teach in a school or a community center." After being escorted through a labyrinth of steel security doors and gates, we made it to C yard. We were escorted into the gym where our classes would be held. Another correctional officer awaited us to give us an orientation. It went something like this, "If you hear the alarm, stand up against the wall. We might need to come rushing in. If we kill one of yours, don't

worry, we'll get you another one." This comment along with other toxic comments included the "gunner" on the catwalk and frequent visits and snarly glares from a guard who participants identified as "the ballbuster" for her proclivity to sucker punch inmates in the groin. Lockdowns interrupted our weekly programming, and dragging in and clubbing hog-tied prisoners and throwing them into a small cage in the corner by the entrance to the gym was a regular occurrence.

I've been working in spaces of confinement for over three decades. Whether in prison or in struggling communities, the questions being asked are the same: How can we create a nurturing, learning, and sharing environment in the face of such stark dehumanizing authoritarian brutality? What potential impacts could our work have in the short and long term? Will that be enough? These and other critical questions always lead me back to my beginnings.

I grew up in a family of people who cared deeply about justice. My grandparents, aunties, uncles, and parents were involved in social movements to varying degrees. I was born in Salinas, California, in 1973. My mom moved us to Los Angeles in 1976 so that she could fulfill her role as cochair of the defense committee for Paul Skyhorse and Richard Mohawk, two American Indian Movement (AIM) members who were on trial for murder. The trial had been moved from Ventura County to Los Angeles. My dad moved to LA to join the August 29th Movement, a Marxist-Leninist organization that was born out of the 1970 Chicano Moratorium. My parents divorced that same year. In 1978, the August 29th Movement merged with I Wor Kuen, East Wind Collective, Seize the Time Collective, the New York Collective, and finally the Revolutionary Communist League to form the League of Revolutionary Struggle (which lasted from 1978 to 1989). Both of my parents were part of this organization. My mom left the organization in 1983 primarily because of the inability of its leadership to include a feminist agenda in its strategic vision and values. Nevertheless, she has remained active until today and raised us as working-class feminists of color.

I fell deeply in love with playing music by the time I was fifteen. This relationship has been incredibly complicated and filled with tensions, contradictions, and recurring moments of belonging. The obligation to uphold the values of my family and community was ever present. It was not and would never be enough to write and perform songs about justice, struggle, and movement. Nor would it be acceptable to keep the practice of music compartmentalized and absent of community. My experience of being a musician in the music industry was often extractive and transactional: signing record contracts, recording albums (albeit about social justice), bouncing from one city to another performing, doing countless interviews for newspapers, TV, and radio, building a fan base, creating the sensational illusion

Poster designed by Rachael Romero, San Francisco Poster Brigade, 1977. Linoleum cut; sheet: 22 7/16 × 17 5/16 inches (57 × 44 cm), https://www.loc.gov/resource/ppmsca.43322/.

that somehow we were "making it." The reality was that we were often exhausted, broke, with no health insurance, and ultimately being told that in order for us to get to the "next level" upward, we were required to "leave our community behind." Simultaneously and in between these difficult moments, there were moments of incredible connection and emergence. Born out of these moments are theories, methodologies, frameworks, and practices that have supported us in being able to land in community with cultural practice and in cultural practice with community. One of these methodologies and theoretical frameworks is outward mobility.

Outward mobility as a methodology can be understood as individual and collective lateral movements out of the way of harm from the dominant structure into spaces of imagination and possibilities, leveraging deeply rooted traditional cultural practices sustained and innovated upon in BIPOC communities as vehicles for transporting us outward, where we intentionally propagate interwoven, sustainable, and cooperative systems and structures for now and for future generations. As a theoretical framework, outward mobility is a collective mirror by which we can look at the most simplistic or complex cultural practice and find beauty, belonging, connection, and an inherent community accountability. Access to this mobility requires critical cultural shifts away from perpetual reactive modes of resistance and into ones of regeneration where many work together to will an emergent "world where many worlds fit."

It was a warm October 2022 evening at Salazar Park in East LA. After being socially distanced for over two years, we took the advice of the Inner-City Muslim Action Network and applied social connection with safe physical distancing. This was the first time the Community Power Collective held our LiderArte leadership development program in person. Margarita, Eva, and I, the Community Power Collective's cultural team, had prepared for months in collaboration with the CONTRA-TIEMPO activist dance theater. La Señora Maria cooked lentejas, tacos de papa, and fruta picada. Her food would always put us in the right frame of mind, body, and spirit.

Ana Maria opened the workshop with CONTRA-TIEMPO's signature Mi Cuerpo practice. "Llamada y respuesta! [call and response]. *Esto es mi cuerpo!* Esto es mi cuerpo. *No es de el!* No es de el! *Ni de ellos!* Ni de ellos! *Es solo mio!* Es solo mio!" This practice of reclamation of body was part of the central theme of this iteration of programming called "Movimiento para el Movimiento." Movement for the Movement. The participants for this session were all monolingual Spanish-speaking, immigrant women. Most were experiencing housing insecurity or homelessness, and some were street vendors who had been fighting for a dignified work environment without persecution from the cops, city, or county.

"LiderArte" poster, CP Collective and Contra-Tiempo, 2022. Reprinted with permission.

The previous week, Jannet led us through the dances of the Orishas including Oshun. As a follow-up, Ana Maria prompted a dialogue in the opening circle with an intriguing question, "Holding up the mirror of Oshun, what do you see that you love?" Everyone lifted up their hands, staring into their palms as if they were mirrors, and took a moment to reflect on the question. "I've never been asked this before." Pause. "I love my eyes. They are very expressive," shared one señora. Another said, "It's taken me a long time to say this . . . I love my curvy body." The next señora said, "I love that I fight for justice." Around it went like wildfire, señoras sharing and affirming a love of self in community through cultural practice. When it got to the final señora, her eyes welled up and she shook her head to signify that she was unable to share. Now, in a moment like this, my tendency is to deflect attention away from the person to support their need to not feel pressure. Suddenly, "I love your beautiful brown skin!" shouted one señora. "I love your kindness. You always make me feel welcome." Even the women who didn't know her were sharing affirmations.

In an effort to make ourselves whole again, we consciously and subconsciously reach toward ancestral technologies.

What happened with the señoras is not new, but part of a continuum of cultural practices that spans thousands of years in Indigenous, African, and other traditional communities. In many ways, the impacts of colonialism and white supremacist capitalist patriarchy have left us individually and collectively fractured. Still, in an effort to make ourselves whole again, we consciously and subconsciously reach toward ancestral technologies. The women came to each other and affirmed when they needed each other most. These systems of repair and transformation are both the vehicles and the path that help to transport us outward, outside of the values of white supremacist capitalist patriarchy and into new imaginaries where we can, with new behaviors, new language, and new understandings, build sustainable interconnected structures. In this particular case, it was a move from tension and dammed-up emotions to a release into a community embrace that is also the collective action.

August 2023. I got a text that said we needed to have an emergency Zoom meeting regarding one of the coalition partners who was evicting seven families. This was obviously unacceptable for a coalition built to push back against displacement and gentrification. The other coalition members were lining up to urge them to reconsider their eviction process. I logged in and was trying to prepare what I thought might be a generative offering. The Zoom opened and each representative from their respective organizations filed in. Most everyone had their cameras on. The meeting opened with a community member giving testimony about the

historic and ongoing practices of this organization with its tenants. The president of the organization explained, "We are in the nonprofit housing business. This is the system we're working in and sometimes this is going to happen." Thinking about how that response didn't sit well, I responded, "You are also operating in a community of color. This community has a moral system that you are accountable to." All nonprofit developers are operating in a fixed system of building affordable housing that holds them in line, beholden to wealthy investors and the general real estate and urban development game. But let's apply outward mobility for a second and say that my offering ignited an imaginary of our community's shared values and practices, that this organization would hold itself accountable by leveraging the moral resources to find regenerative responses to the situation. Let's say that they decide to adopt and implement a no-eviction policy. Instead, they are going to invest in programmatic structures that will support tenants experiencing difficulties paying their rent or adhering to the rules of the buildings. These programs are, at their core, designed to repair, restore, and transform not only the individual or family in question but the entirety of the tenants. Let's take it a step further and say that in building these capacities organizationally, they are outwardly mobile enough to see the need to build out collective ownership models with the tenants. And on and on and on . . . I'm not naive; I'm a dreamer.

Taking a step back and critically analyzing each of the three stories I shared, we can see that there are two diametrically opposed parallel cultural systems at play. One is a supremacy culture that is predicated on absolute domination and violence in order for one small group of people to leverage power over a large group of vulnerable people in pursuit of the fallacy of moving "upward." Whether it is a person in a cell behind prison walls or in the hood or barrio, an exploited worker or unemployed person, a renter who is in danger of being evicted, an immigrant, a woman, a queer or trans person, the disabled, or those discarded for being too old to produce labor, this supremacy cultural system keeps the majority confined to a particular location, behavior, social status. The other system is a culture of accompaniment, improvisation, imagination, participation, and collective critical self-reflection. Participants in prison and in community spaces have often described the impacts of these systems as a "a piece of freedom," "magic," and "healing." These moments of freedom are an example of a civic media generated by cultural traditions, some old, some more recent. All of them emerge from cultural communities of practice. Embedded in these practices are vehicles and road maps toward moments of clarity outside of the mental, spiritual, and physical stronghold of the corrupted, corroded, and collapsing structure. It's these moments that allow us to plant seeds, cultivate symbiotic ecosystems, and imagine and actively pursue a dignified future.

Conjuring Community in Apocalyptic Times

A Winding Road Map on Facilitating Diverse Groups for Collaboration

Michelle Zenarosa

Michelle Zenarosa (she/they) has almost twenty years of experience in journalism and media making through a social justice lens, having worked at various news outlets, including *Fusion*, *Everyday Feminism*, *New America Media*, and *LA Weekly*, and is currently editor in chief at *LA Public Press*. Previously, they were the community manager at USC's Annenberg Innovation Lab, where they curated the Civic Media Fellowship. She has been a facilitator for storytelling by youth in Los Angeles, Washington, DC, and Palestine and was awarded the 2017 Society of Features Journalism Fellowship. She's a grouchy ex-punk and is serious about her snacks.

First things first: Facilitation is not for the faint of heart.

Facilitation is definitely a superpower, but the role of a facilitator is often undervalued and misunderstood. In groups, a good facilitator can be the linchpin between disastrous chaos and triumphant collaboration.

Even in the best scenarios, it's really hard. But when it's happening in a tornado of institutionalized white supremacy and multiple deadly global crises, it's treacherous.

At least it definitely felt that way for me at times, as I held the role of fellowship facilitator and curator for the Civic Media Fellowship for over three years. At one point, the challenge was so intense that I had to take a three-month sabbatical.

When I took the job in the second half of 2019, I was not really a trained facilitator. With almost two decades of experience as a newsroom leader and journalist, my strength lay in facilitating storytelling, not orchestrating the dynamics of large to midsize groups for community building and transformative leadership.

What I didn't know then that I know now is that a facilitator, in this context, is not like a conductor dictating to the orchestra, but like a gardener tending fertile ground. The soil is the bedrock of clear expectations, the essential starting point. The facilitator's work begins with tilling this ground, painstakingly removing the weeds of confusion, distrust, and the deep-seated trauma that can poison collaboration. From this carefully tended soil, diverse voices begin to emerge and bloom. This blossoming starts with a powerful investment in the community within the fellowship, creating a safe space for connection and shared purpose. But the flowering doesn't stop there. It sends out ripples, connecting these individual communities to each other, creating a network of shared resources and amplified impact. Even the inevitable lightning strikes of tension and disagreement become part of the process, fertilizing the ground for even greater innovation and more effective solutions.

Did I fully do this and succeed? No, but hindsight's twenty-twenty, and I now have a road map to get me closer to that ideal. I'm also able to name the major factors that got in the way and that potentially get in the way for anyone facilitating working teams within this capitalist hellscape we live in. Ideally you can do this without financial constraints from funders, universities, the nonprofit industrial complex, and so on, but if you have to work within them, I have some lessons to share.

It's important to say from the outset that "civic media" is a term coined by straight, white men in academia. Media scholar and USC professor Henry Jenkins, who was a cofounder of the Civic Media Fellowship, is often credited with popularizing the term in the mid-2000s. His 2006 book *Convergence Culture* and subsequent writing extensively explored the concept, defining it as "any use of any medium which fosters or enhances civic engagement." And although he didn't coin the term, Ethan Zuckerman, the former longtime director of the MIT Center for Civic Media, also significantly contributed to solidifying its meaning, demonstrating its real-world applications, and advocating for its responsible development.

Why is this relevant? The majority of Civic Media fellows were people of color, many LGBTQ, and all were engaged in critical work challenging powerful institutions. Some held toxic relationships with academia, stemming from its historical exclusion and biases rooted in white supremacy. These factors shaped how relationships unfolded within the fellowship, both among fellows and with the full-time staff, nearly all of whom were white. It was a recipe for discontent.

The apocalypse was here. There was COVID-19, the uprisings following George Floyd, the earth simultaneously on fire and under water, and no one being able to afford anything. This particular moment was arguably the largest culture shift in our lifetime, significantly altering the way we think about how we live, work, shop, and take care of our kids.

For many of the folks in the fellowship, leaders in their community, the program itself was a container to hold all of those things for the ten months that they were together regularly. I personally made a ton of mistakes and missteps. I also learned a lot along the way.

Because of my own lived experience as a queer daughter of undocumented parents, I knew I had to look to experts that I felt aligned with my worldview and those of the fellows. So I vigorously read and took notes from writer and activist adrienne maree brown's *Holding Change*; I consulted with AORTA, a worker-owned cooperative that facilitates antioppressive practices and structures within social justice movements; and I did trainings with Training for Change, a nonprofit focusing on training and capacity building for activists and organizers working in social justice movements. I also attended the Allied Media Conference, as I had done years before, but this time with new eyes, looking specifically toward group facilitation. My framework on facilitation is grounded in this blend of lived experience, theoretical underpinnings, and practical tools from all of these teachers.

While my experience at USC serves as a case study, I recognize the broader reality: Many of us working in historically inequitable spaces find ourselves trapped in a paradox. We end up reproducing the very same toxic power dynamics and funding

structures we aim to dismantle. I know this shouldn't be the case, but I also confront the harsh truth: Securing funding within these systems typically involves navigating difficult choices and maneuvering among uncomfortable compromises.

Despite these constraints, there are still many valuable lessons that can be learned from being together in this particular moment. Here are some hard-won, practical insights I learned, applied, and sometimes stumbled through:

1. Construct Strong Containers

What's a container? This is a question that I and others had after several fellows with organizing experience in Black movement spaces repeatedly referred to creating containers for the group.

I learned that containers are metaphorical spaces created to hold and support difficult conversations and collective action around any issues arising in the group. It's not a physical room, but rather the atmosphere, agreements, and practices that guide the group's interactions. Building these spaces was the first thing we needed to do to be able to move forward with intention, principle, and care.

The two biggest containers we created together were around defining goals and community agreements, which basically helped us define what it meant to come together as a group.

The fellowship—as is the case with many group projects—did not have the luxury of planning beforehand; it was a build-the-airplane-as-you-fly mentality. Because of that, it was important to set some goals and ground rules at the start.

There was some tension with this: Some staff felt that we shouldn't have rules or guidelines because they would limit fellows' imagination and participation. So we tried that, and it didn't work. Without those guiding elements, people felt lost.

One of the fellows—who I won't name to keep our conversation private—said something particularly poignant: She found it extraordinarily jarring and stressful to approach the fellowship without a clear set of goals and community agreements, that in particular, as a Black queer woman—and this echoed sentiments from other BIPOC folks—she had learned to survive by "getting good grades" in school. She wanted to know how to get an A and she wanted to know that she was doing the fellowship "right."

Navigating the fellowship without those things felt like shaky ground, and if you don't feel the ground firmly under your feet, it is undeniable that you will fall. This was a major lesson we learned as we got up from our initial falls.

Forging a shared identity became another crucial element in shaping the fellowship container. Initially, terms like "civic media maker" and "creative"

swirled around, but a sense of common ground remained elusive. Finding the thread that wove our diverse practices together became a priority.

Ultimately, there wasn't a uniform term that was officially agreed upon, but when one of the fellows brought up the work of Favianna Rodriguez—interdisciplinary artist and activist and cofounder of the Center for Cultural Power—the term "cultural worker" stuck.

Cultural workers, Rodriguez asserts, are the midwives of social change, using their art and artistry to challenge the status quo and inspire new visions of possibility. Cultural workers operate at the intersection of art, culture, and activism, using their creative and critical faculties to challenge power structures and inspire collective action.

Later, we were privileged to invite Emory Douglas, the revolutionary artist and minister of culture for the Black Panther Party. His work served as a North Star for some of the fellows and further solidified the term "cultural worker" as a label that resonated.

Those two were big-picture containers, but we can't overstate the importance of building smaller, regular containers, which for us were feedback channels—places where folks could feel like they could chime in and let us know if it was working or not and what their needs were. Any time that you could find ways to let folks know where they could lead, provide insight, and gain ownership of the fellowship was a major victory.

Cultural workers are the midwives of social change.

2. Look to Emergent Strategies

In *Holding Change*, adrienne maree brown offers a framework for navigating the complexities of social justice work in times of uncertainty. She advocates for *emergent strategies*, approaches that are adaptable, responsive, and grounded in the lived experiences of those most affected by injustice.

Whether we intended to or not, we had to use emergent strategies to navigate the ever-shifting landscape of disaster and disruption. We engaged in them countless times throughout the fellowship, in both good and challenging moments—such as dealing with the loss of parents, miscarriages, divorces, and financial trauma. As a facilitator, it was crucial for me to use radical listening skills, responding as issues and themes surfaced during our time together.

One of the biggest moments to recall was after COVID-19 hit in March 2020, six months after I joined the team. While the pandemic raged on, and the government predictably failed us, we were told to stock up, stay apart, and fend for ourselves.

During this same period, the deaths of George Floyd and Breonna Taylor brought up intense trauma and anger for fellows who were reckoning with some hard truths about the political and cultural choices made and the leaders we elected.

In this period the extended fellowship network got tighter while at the same time demanding much more from the space. We fumbled our way around, trying to make our regular calls a fun and generative space so that folks could find inspiration and nurture their creativity, but what they also really wanted was a space for reflection on the innumerable losses we'd experienced personally and collectively, and the ways in which we'd made it through.

Thanks to the fellow who explicitly asked for this space in a private conversation with me, we were able to invite senior fellow Carla Fernandez and her team at The Dinner Party, a platform for grieving adults to find real community and build lasting relationships, to lead a guided reflection on "our losses and what powers us through."

Poet and media activist Malkia Devich-Cyril, in her writings on grief as a catalyst for change, proposes that embracing grief can be a potent force for social transformation. She argues that grief, when acknowledged and processed, can fuel the collective will to challenge injustice and build a more just world.

It was a tremendous assignment for me as a facilitator to show up for the hard conversations. The long session with The Dinner Party was not a cure-all, but it was enough to let the fellows feel seen and to emphasize the importance of acknowledging and inviting grief into our space—a lesson that using an emergent strategy taught us.

3. Get Comfortable with Conflict

Just kidding, I lied. Conflict is usually uncomfortable and that's okay. And I won't lie again, this was the part of the job I was most unprepared for.

Less than halfway through my tenure, I learned about American psychological researcher Bruce Tuckman's concept of the "storming" stage of group development. It was almost like clockwork: As each cohort delved deeper into the program, sometime around the midpoint of the fellowship the initial harmony gave way to inevitable disagreements.

Tuckman's stages of group development describes the five stages that groups typically go through as they develop: forming, storming, norming, performing, and adjourning. According to Tuckman, each stage has its own unique characteristics and challenges, and effective group leaders need to be able to identify and address the needs of their groups at each stage.

For us at the fellowship, each time a conflict or tension would arise would be different—it could be around race and class or around the discomfort with white staff or even around financial trauma and intellectual property. And on top of these tensions, the hierarchical nature of an elite university institution made it feel nearly impossible to fully feel safe enough to challenge the status quo and facilitate open and honest communication across all levels of the hierarchy.

What if we approached conflict as an opportunity to learn?

Getting a bunch of bold people like the fellows together on a yearlong adventure was always going to get messy, but the first time it came to a head on my watch was hard. There were multiple unresolved ruptures across various relationships, and we could not figure out how to repair them enough to make it feel safe enough for people to continue showing up day to day at the fellowship.

None of us on staff felt equipped to mediate, especially when some of the conflict was with staff, so we hired a social justice–oriented consulting and coaching firm, Freedom Verses. They helped us create a framework for coming together to create braver spaces that we were able to replicate to some degree.

We never got to a place where it felt like moving through conflict was easy or even successful, but the lessons we learned along the way were still valuable, especially since we knew it was always going to show up. So, what if we approached conflict as an opportunity to learn? As an opportunity to get closer through vulnerability?

4. Build Trust in Large and Small Ways

Another one of the biggest obstacles as a facilitator was getting folks to collaborate. The vision of the fellowship was built on the dream of getting a bunch of brilliant people from different disciplines together not just to learn but to build and create. Hopefully after getting to know one another, fellows could be inspired to break out into small groups or pairs and experiment or work on projects together.

This of course is easier said than done, and we often struggled with it.

I often asked fellows what would help them collaborate, and one response in particular resonated with me. A fellow said, "I only like to make stuff with my friends, and I don't feel like these folks are my friends." He was spot on. There just wasn't enough trust to work together. So how do you do that in a few months and virtually?

I immediately got to work, adding a number of remixed team-building activities. I also built in more one-on-one time, matching fellows together by utilizing a magical combination of radical listening, paying attention to group dynamics, and connecting individual stories to the group's purpose. Did I know that a fellow was trying to quit their job? Well then I'm matching them with one who quit their job last year. Was an artist thinking about having a baby? I'm matching them with another parent artist. It was a little more complicated than that sometimes, but the point is, I always had my ear out and spidey senses on to see who could make connections with each other. I also held semiregular speed dating sessions for collaboration to jumpstart teamwork.

In our time together, we also learned how to balance and fine-tune when to take risks together—when did sharing vulnerability feel good and when did it feel too heavy? How could we create moments that were more light touch but invited folks to get deeper, if they wanted to? We asked fellows to create short life maps and five-minute presentations to fellows to connect on a personal level and discover shared interests or passions. We planned fun projects like a recipe book with stories and listened for serendipitous opportunities to share our lives, like when we all shared the artwork in our homes on Zoom.

This also meant I was building in moments for imagination and play—another critical piece of the puzzle. In social justice spaces, there is a dominant narrative that people must always be toiling, fighting, and struggling. We had to combat that narrative because so much of what we were seeing was depressing, stressful, and chaotic, wrecking our nervous systems and releasing chemicals in our body to make us freeze. Just as much as folks were bringing to light the nightmares, they had to be sharing narratives that illuminated their dreams, their joys, and their power.

We did a comic book. We did a cookbook. We made Muslim Valentine cards. We hung out with baby goats. We did virtual karaoke. We made pasta together with grandmas in Italy on Zoom. We played drag queen bingo. We invited a dream maker and astrologist to lead daydreaming and reading sessions with the group. Fellows also led their own imaginative, future, and world-building sessions.

Was it all sunshine and rainbows? No, not everyone found their BFFs (although a few did!) or jumped into joint projects headfirst. While a full-fledged, deep-rooted trust network couldn't be perfectly woven in just nine months, the seeds planted did sprout in many ways.

In the fall of 2023, for instance, a whole bunch of fellows took the initiative without staff to team up to organize art projects around the Palestinian genocide. At the beginning of the project one messaged me privately, "Who do you trust here?" That trust had to continuously be reinforced, but it was totally worth it.

And that, perhaps, is the greatest triumph of all—witnessing the ripples of connection spread outward, leaving a legacy of collaboration long after the fellowship came to a close. I suspect we'll continue to see those ripples years from now.

5. Cultivate a Culture of Radical Self-Care

Lastly, it cannot go unstated that during their time with us, most fellows—all of whom are flag bearers and trailblazers in their communities—had been recovering from or in the middle of extreme burnout.

It's no secret that folks working in the space of social change often put all their energy into it, devoting many hours to their work, often with little or no space for breaks. Many are a source of strength for their community, often sacrificing a lot to support those they care about and for whom they fight alongside.

All of this takes a toll—mentally, physically, emotionally. We heard this from our fellows again and again, and there was no way to spend almost a year together without acknowledging and addressing this reality. So what could people do to take care of themselves and each other in this kind of warped fellowship space under the auspices of USC? And how could civic media be redefined to recognize the needs of visionaries suffering from burnout?

We initially experimented with a potent session I led around unpacking imposter syndrome and inviting a USC mindfulness practitioner, who was a white man, to lead a mindful creativity workshop. It was . . . weird and it didn't really get to the root of the problem.

In our next iteration, we invited Allissa Richardson, USC faculty and author of *Bearing Witness While Black: African Americans, Smartphones, and the New Protest #Journalism*, to lead a ninety-minute self-care session with the fellows. She was piloting a comprehensive self-care curriculum that encompassed everything from intellectual and spiritual self-care to financial and emotional self-care. Once she did one session, we quickly realized it needed to be a yearlong thing and it needed to be permanent. Bearing witness to each other's self-care within the group was powerful, and thanks to Allissa, we all took many lessons with us that we will carry forever.

As a facilitator, one major lesson that we learned when practicing radical self-care as a group is to be intentional about who is in the space. Unnecessary moments of mistrust and pain bubbled up when we weren't careful about making sure everyone in the space was being fully vulnerable and there were no voyeurs. It was uncomfortable as a facilitator to gently push white staff to take a step back and stop attending these especially sacred circles, but ultimately it was better for the group.

The second major lesson around self-care was brought on when a fellow posed a simple but game-changing question: How do you maintain hope? This was a question that was incredibly important in that moment and one we were constantly asking ourselves in the midst of one disaster after another.

Doing this work requires rigorous hope—an unwavering belief in the capacity for human transformation.

I was honored to invite to the fellowship the prophetic Tricia Hersey, founder of The Nap Ministry, and the prescient abolitionist organizer and educator Mariame Kaba to speak with the fellows. Tricia taught us to rest as an act of defiance against oppressive systems that exploit and exhaust marginalized communities, particularly Black people. Mariame reminded us that while suffering and inhumanity exist, so too do compassion, kindness, and selflessness. She taught us that hope is not something you have but something that you do and something you practice daily and commit to.

Fundamentally, we learned together that doing this work requires rigorous hope—an unwavering belief in the capacity for human transformation to make better worlds free from oppression. As a facilitator, it was my job to find ways to champion hope as a discipline.

I can reflect now that what we did together to take care of ourselves and each other during the fellowship in all its messiness and stressfulness was something worth celebrating. And in the long run, for my mistakes, "Never a failure, always a lesson."

Claiming
and
Reclaiming

Civic Media

A Space for Exploration

Sue Ding

Sue Ding (she/her) is a filmmaker and visual artist based in Los Angeles. Her work explores race, gender, and diaspora through the lens of visual culture and place-based storytelling. Sue's work has screened at SXSW, IDFA, and True/False, and can be found on platforms including PBS, Netflix, and *The New York Times*. Her interdisciplinary practice spans film, installation, and emerging media, emphasizing process, form, and deep readings of both media and landscapes. She also consults and lectures widely on nonfiction filmmaking and participatory storytelling. In 2023, she was named one of *Filmmaker* magazine's 25 New Faces of Independent Film.

Artists from marginalized communities face enormous challenges, including structural barriers, erasure, and harmful narratives. Speaking from the margins, we are well versed in finding alternative strategies of communication—storytelling against the grain to create counternarratives and new language to reflect our experiences. Yet the current media ecosystem often pressures us to restrict ourselves to certain types of stories and certain modes of praxis. In light of these hurdles, the nascent and fundamentally interdisciplinary field of civic media offers an essential space for people and projects that are category-defying, shape-shifting, and multifaceted—and that consequently often struggle to find support or community elsewhere.

Writing from the perspective of an artist and documentary filmmaker, I want to emphasize both the importance of this type of work and the obstacles creators encounter in making it.

In our current cultural landscape, people representing marginalized perspectives are all too often required to mold their stories into a specific shape in order to obtain funding and visibility. Narrative conventions are designed to be legible and nonthreatening to a mainstream audience assumed to be white, straight, cisgender, nondisabled, and normative in every sense.

In the documentary world, that often means a three-act linear structure, a heroic protagonist, and above all, a story of oppression that is designed to edify but also to reassure. Audiences are presented with a happy ending or a simplistic call to action, and are rarely asked to confront their own privilege in any meaningful way. We are told that such films engender empathy in viewers by "humanizing" their subjects. Beyond the question of what empathy alone can actually accomplish, this framework presupposes that the intended audiences and the communities portrayed in the films are mutually exclusive—upholding voyeuristic and paternalistic elements that have been present in the documentary field since its inception.

Meanwhile, initiatives ostensibly designed to support marginalized creators—grants, fellowships, incubators, and so on—often inadvertently generate new constraints and obstacles. Artists are asked to perform trauma, flatten complex stories

and characters, and dramatize conflict in ways that are driven by market imperatives as well as a narrow conception of equity and representation.

A casual perusal of current grant opportunities for QTPOC filmmakers yields mentions of "critical issues," "resistance," "impact," "moral urgency," and "changing the world." Resistance against what? Urgency for whom? Who gets to define what these terms mean? Gatekeepers, who remain a primarily white and socioeconomically homogeneous group, profess their support for diverse stories. However, they frequently exacerbate the burdens of representation by reducing creators to a series of checked boxes—a yes/no assessment of oppression—rather than allowing them to express the full complexity of their lived experiences.

We *all* represent intersectional identities, and experience joy and community alongside struggle. We all have stories that may not follow a linear path or arrive at an easy resolution. How can we truly uplift marginalized voices if we only allow them the limited canvas of conventional narrative and the limited palette of trauma? The stakes are considerable not only for artists but also for society as a whole: Impoverishing the images we see of ourselves also diminishes our ability to imagine emancipatory, visionary, and radical futures.

What can civic media offer to ease these concerns? This burgeoning field is a vital space for creators who seek to challenge narrative norms and explore new forms of media making. As a relatively new area, and one that is inherently interdisciplinary, it is perhaps less beholden to received wisdom and more open to questioning assumptions about storytelling, audience, and authorship. And as a field that itself is still being defined, it welcomes bold experimentation and a spirit of exploration that emphasizes process as much as results.

Civic media practitioners do the crucial work of disrupting dominant narratives not only by offering insightful critiques and alternative storylines, but also by imagining new and expansive forms of storytelling. Their work may not have clearly defined authors, plots, or endings. They embrace the discursive, in form and process—ongoing conversations rather than neat endings, open-ended questions rather than didactic lessons. Their projects may be books and interactive games and performances all at once, dynamically exploring the affordances and limitations of multiple formats.

Examples of fluid, multifaceted, and fantastically creative projects abound in past and present Civic Media Fellowship cohorts.

Black Miami-Dade, founded by Nadege Green, describes itself as "a multimedia history and storytelling platform that resists the erasure of Miami-Dade County's Black past." The research-based initiative spans a website, social media, and in-person events. For the exhibit *Give Them Their Flowers*, Green and Marie

Installation view of *Give Them Their Flowers* at Little Haiti Cultural Center Art Gallery, Miami. Copyright © David Gary Lloyd Photography.

Building Utopia Deck, https://www.buildingutopiadeck.com/. Courtesy of Dr. Christina Harrington and Jennifer S. Roberts.

Vickles curated historical images, artifacts, and contemporary artwork celebrating Miami's queer Black past. Green also conducted oral history interviews with queer elders in the community, filling in gaps in the historical record. This multimodal and restorative approach explores different ways of both engaging with history and crafting new narratives in the face of erasure.

Building Utopia, created by Jennifer S. Roberts, Christina Harrington, Kirsten Bray, and N'Deye Diakhate, is "an Afrofuturism-inspired toolkit." This set of card decks (with accompanying guidebook) offers an accessible introduction to speculative design strategies, with an emphasis on Black liberation and marginalized groups. Used at community events and creative workshops, they act as a framework for participants to create their own narratives and to imagine radical futures for themselves and their communities.

In my own work, I am passionate about exploring new approaches to storytelling, across projects spanning film, installation, and emerging media. *One Square Mile, 10,000 Voices*, which I created together with Halsey Burgund, is an interactive documentary, participatory oral history project, location-based experience, and audio-augmented reality installation exploring the legacy of Japanese American incarceration during World War II.

In 1942, the United States government forced 120,000 men, women, and children to leave their homes and detained them in harsh and remote incarceration camps. More than 10,000 Japanese Americans were held at Manzanar War Relocation Center in California, now a national historic site. *One Square Mile* layers voices from Manzanar's past and present over the physical landscape, both at Manzanar and in Los Angeles's Little Tokyo neighborhood.

We geolocated brief audio recordings—oral history interviews with Japanese American and Paiute-Shoshone elders, WWII news reports, recordings of recent memorials and protests—across these sites. Using a mobile device and headphones, visitors are immersed in a soundscape that responds dynamically to their movement: Based on where they walk and where they stop to listen, each person's experience is unique. Halsey and I hoped to craft an experience that was meditative, embodied, and exploratory, as opposed to more traditionally didactic presentations.

As visitors wander, they can also record their own voices and stories to add to the project, building a living document of resistance, resilience, and community across generations. This participatory storytelling approach invites conversation surrounding not only the injustice Japanese Americans faced during WWII, but also how it connects to contemporary issues affecting visitors' lives, including immigration and gentrification. And it suggests that we regard historical injustice not simply as part of a static past, but rather as part of an ongoing process of struggle and solidarity.

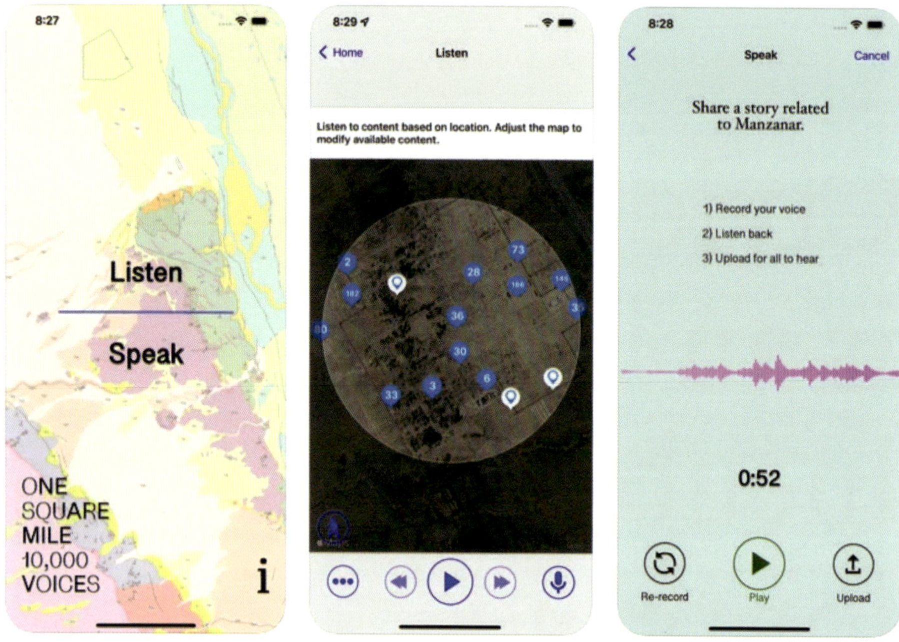

One Square Mile, 10,000 Voices, 2022, https://onesquaremile.fm/. Copyright © Sue Ding and Halsey Burgund.

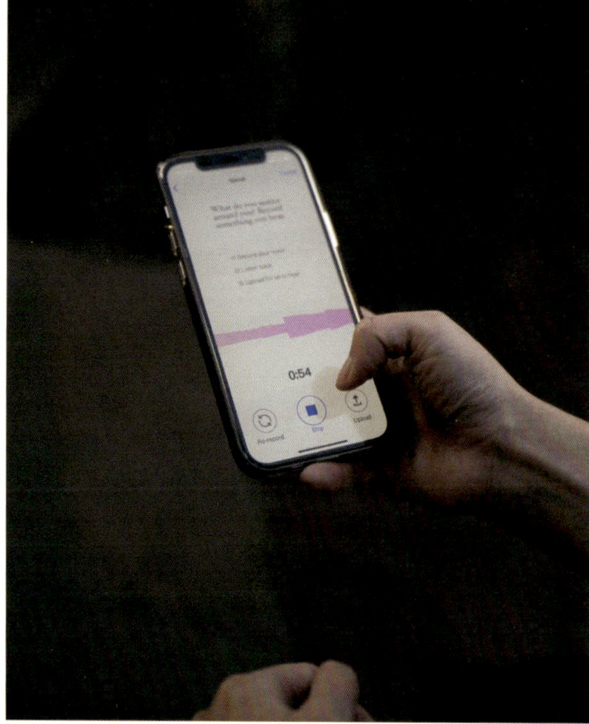

Users experiencing *One Square Mile, 10,000 Voices*, Los Angeles, 2022. Photos by Justin Chu, courtesy of Visual Communications Photographic Archive. Reprinted with permission.

Civic media is an ideal incubation space for projects that aim to generate interaction and conversation across both social and spatial boundaries.

Civic media operates as an important space for fostering these types of projects, which can struggle to acquire the same support and visibility as more traditional work. Funders and distributors often prefer projects that are more straightforward in both form and content, hewing to the proven track record of past successes. Of course, success according to an institutional or market perspective can be defined in ways that may or may not align with artists' priorities and values.

In addition to constraints regarding what stories we tell and how we tell them, navigating the broader media ecosystem presents its own challenges. There remains an enormous lack of transparency, access, and equity in media, despite some progress in recent years. Beyond these overarching structural problems, existing frameworks present particular difficulties for people working across different media and within multiple contexts.

Market forces drive creators to specialize, racking up accolades in specific areas. Documentary filmmakers, for example, might focus on academic spaces, network television, public media, mainstream film festivals, galleries and museums, social platforms, experimental venues, or international markets. Projects can and do exist in multiple arenas—successful feature documentaries often premiere on the festival circuit and then move on to a public television broadcast or streaming platform. But creators typically must build up specialized expertise, networks, and name recognition in order to gain access to each new space. This is no small task, especially for independent artists without an agent, distributor, or other support.

Thus, the simplest option for many people is to focus on one or two main arenas. This, however, limits the types of audiences their work is exposed to, as well as the discourses it participates in. After many years of creating and viewing work primarily in academia, for example, a filmmaker might become accustomed to that field's prevalent forms, habitual criticisms, and assumption of shared reference points. They might operate in an increasingly narrow context, rather than exploring new modes of collaboration, production, and distribution.

There is of course nothing wrong with crafting work for a specific audience or developing expertise within a specific context, and there are many benefits to doing so (particularly when it comes to groups who have long been ignored in mainstream spaces). However, for creators whose work can be difficult to pinpoint, and who operate across multiple disciplines and registers, this framework can be deeply frustrating. There are countless projects that struggle to find support because they are too unwieldy for the narrow confines of existing categories: too experimental for the mainstream film festival, not academic enough for the conference circuit, too complex to be confined to one platform.

Yet these works, beyond their artistic merit, also play a vital role in expanding how we think about media. They challenge assumptions about how work is authored, how audiences interact with a project, and how categories themselves are defined and assigned. In traversing different fields, they can bring together a wide and sometimes unexpected range of stakeholders.

With civic media's inherent focus on publics and discourses, as well as its interdisciplinary nature, it is an ideal incubation space for projects that aim to generate interaction and conversation across both social and spatial boundaries. In looking at the work of past and current Civic Media fellows, it's clear that there is a desire to work beyond narrowly defined disciplines and media platforms.

FLOAT Beijing, by Xiaowei Wang and Deren Guler, was a series of workshops and public performances conducted in 2012. Addressing Beijing's air pollution as well as its censorship of air quality data, the team worked with residents to create and fly specially designed kites. These kites were equipped with pollution-detecting sensors, as well as color-coded LED lights indicating specific particulate levels. At night, an array of brightly lit kites appeared in the sky, transmitting current air quality conditions to all below. FLOAT combines urban design, public art, and citizen science. It also brought artists, technologists, and local citizens together in a form of dialogue with the Chinese government, pressuring officials to publicly release air quality data (they began doing so a few months after the project took place).

Arshia Fatima Haq's project Discostan, a "diasporic discotheque," is a record label, a roving dance party, and an ongoing social practice project. Featuring kaleidoscopic visuals and music from South and West Asia and North Africa (SWANA), as well as live performances and artistic collaborations, it serves as a showcase for a wide range of music and performers. It is also a celebratory communal space for QTPOC of the SWANA region, a platform and organizing hub for political engagement, and an expansive archival research project unearthing and reimagining collective histories.

My project *One Square Mile, 10,000 Voices*, discussed earlier, combined elements of documentary, oral history, spatial technology, public art, and social practice. It was at once a website, database, mobile app, and site-specific installation. And though the scale of engagement was limited by COVID public health concerns, my cocreator and I were able to collaborate with many communities and organizations in both creating and distributing the project.

We worked with the National Park Service, which administers the Manzanar National Historic Site, to better understand the location and visitor needs, as well as to navigate oral history archives. We learned from the Manzanar Committee, including former detainees and their families, about the legacy of incarceration

FLOAT workshop, Beijing, August 4, 2012. Photos by Elizabeth Phung. Reprinted with permission.

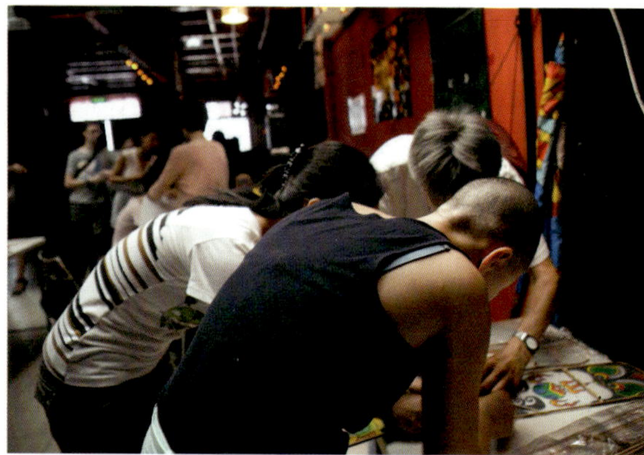

Discostan, Los Angeles, 2018. Photographs by Labkhand Olfatmanesh, courtesy of Arshia Haq and Discostan. Reprinted with permission.

and their ongoing work to support civil rights. We also workshopped versions of the project at MIT's Open Documentary Lab and USC's Annenberg Innovation Lab, and met with CAIR, the Lone Pine Paiute-Shoshone, and Owens Valley environmental activists to learn about Manzanar's layered history and present-day dynamics.

Once completed, we shared the project in venues as disparate as the California League of Park Associations and the Hawaii International Film Festival. While it is rooted in the WWII incarceration of Japanese Americans at Manzanar and other sites across the American West, *One Square Mile* was crafted to connect this legacy with a wide range of contemporary issues and to prompt intersectional discussions among diverse groups. The project attempts to traverse not only different communities and disciplines but also, on some level, time and space. In recording their own stories to add to the project, participants annotate history as well as physical locations, joining in a dynamic exchange with both our pasts and our surroundings.

Our communities, like our identities, are complex and intersectional. Ideally the ecosystem for our work would reflect that reality, rather than forcing us into often arbitrarily (and harmfully) devised categories. But existing structures rarely offer sufficient support for interdisciplinary and multimodal projects. These category-defying efforts offer less certain results than more conventional approaches, but experimentation is crucial—both for artists developing new work and for a society addressing daunting challenges.

As an emerging field that is still in flux, civic media offers a rare space for creators who are forging new paths and working across boundaries. Civic media practitioners craft new forms, imagine radical futures, and encourage us all to shed old assumptions and paradigms. In this nascent moment, I encourage us to embrace more expansive and malleable definitions, including definitions of civic media itself. I call for a civic media that emphasizes the discursive rather than the didactic, and the messiness of reality rather than the neatness of conventional narrative. And I hope that more support for work that is multidimensional, experimental, and open-ended will lead to more sustainable, inspired, and inspiring futures for us all.

Civic Media and the Ethic of Care

Josie Duffy Rice

Josie Duffy Rice (she/her) is a journalist, writer, law school graduate, and podcast host whose work is primarily focused on prosecutors, prisons, and other criminal justice issues. She is the host of the podcast *Unreformed: The Story of the Alabama Industrial School for Negro Children*, released in January 2023, which she also cowrote. She also hosted the podcasts *Justice in America*, *The Thirty-Year Project*, about the 1994 crime bill, and *Corruption Uncovered*, about police corruption in Kansas City. She is the former president of *The Appeal*, a news publication that publishes original journalism about the criminal justice system. Her writing has been featured in *The New York Times*, *Vanity Fair*, *The New Yorker*, *The Atlantic*, and *Slate*.

At night, when my insomnia is most ruthless, I find myself clicking through scans of old Southern newspapers. I study the headlines of papers in towns I've never heard of, places in south Georgia or middle Tennessee, many of them long gone. I confess that I look mostly for tragedy—stories of prisons and punishment, harm and revenge. Sometimes, I guess, I'm looking for some new dimension of understanding the world today by parsing the details of what was. Other times I'm looking for escape—hoping that by glancing into a different era, I'll somehow will myself to sleep.

Mostly, this exercise provides no revelation. But other times I stumble upon something that sticks with me—that fills in the blanks of something broader, when I feel the apprehension of new questions circling somewhere nearby.

Cahaba, Alabama, is a ghost town now—home to no one and nothing save for a few cemeteries—but for a brief moment, it was more than a pass-through. Back in the 1800s, mansions lined the streets, enslaved people worked the fields, and a railroad slithered through the town center. Cahaba was Alabama's first state capital, the epitome of a Confederate town, housing the brutal glory of the plantation class. And though it held just a couple thousand people, it was home to more than one newspaper in its relatively short life.

One morning I stumbled upon archives of the *Cahawba Democrat*, a small weekly paper from the 1830s. On August 18, 1838, the paper reprinted a short quote from London journalist Allan Cunningham. It's just a few sentences accompanied by neither headline nor elaboration, but they are words I've come back to again and again: "A newspaper requires as much care as a child. Neglect it for a moment, and no after care can scarcely redeem it," he wrote. "A casual error in the one, is equivalent to a slight sickness in the other . . . from whence, if it recovers, it comes forth maimed and disfigured, shorn of its pristine beauty, and probably so mutilated that the author of its existence can scarcely recognise his own. Want of the dollars occasions a difficulty of breathing, and all these things combined bring on a delirium and death." He concluded with "The parallel between the newspaper and child ends here—for the former there is no future existence."

These sentences, a flash of words near the end of the paper and easily missed, were printed more than twenty years before the town of Cahaba began to fall apart. But eventually, Cahaba went the way of so many other towns before and since, its growth stifled by its own cruelty. During the Civil War, the Confederacy seized and dismantled the railroad, building Castle Morgan prison camp instead, where thousands of Union soldiers eventually took up residence as prisoners of war. The town, which sat on a floodplain at the convergence of two rivers, was prone to disaster—and mosquitoes—and earned a reputation for death and disease. Eventually, though, the local papers closed. The town began to shut down. And when the war ended, Cahaba did too, emptying along with the prison. What wasn't abandoned was destroyed in a flood. As far as I can tell, the town dwindled to nothing, land sitting lonely until it was finally unincorporated more than thirty years ago.

It seems garish to talk about an ethic of care as it relates to something as amorphous and intangible as "the media." Media is one part form, one part practice, one part industry. A symbol, a shorthand, the term we use when we mean information or entertainment or civic life. Care reflects love and connection, emotions that institutions are unable to receive.

Also—at its worst—the media's failures are infinite: the way it fractures us, destroying the already-frayed threads holding people together; how it reduces us through surface stories of policy without community, politics without people, power without accountability. It veers into spectacle, fertile ground where disintegration and cynicism are sown. Almost 40 percent of America says it doesn't trust mass media at all. But perhaps the worst thing the media does is dilute our imagination, shortening the spectrum of possibility. *Maimed and disfigured. Shorn of its pristine beauty.*

Of course the failures of media are informed by the obstacles it faces. Media is in an unfathomable battle for its existence. This fight seems unprecedented, and in some ways it is. But in other ways it is part and parcel of the industry's history. Cunningham himself predicted the end of newspapers centuries ago. The precarity of the field is part of its historical terror.

Still, this moment is particularly rife with devastation. In many ways, we seem to be taking the slow route to defeat, unable to even grasp the dimensions of the battle before the losses are racked up again. A field shrinking week by week, not just infrastructure but colleagues disappearing because of its brutal economic unsustainability. The losses are infinite—generations of knowledge that isn't passed down, stories that are never told. *So mutilated that the author of its existence can scarcely recognize his own.*

The fact that media is often weaponized does not preclude its potential as tool.

It is hard enough to just survive. But there's truth in the opposite as well. Perhaps the only way through this moment is by imagining something truly better.

Cahaba is not a unique story, nor really a tragic one. It was, after all, a slavery town—a bastion of abuse and white supremacy. And as far as I can tell, there's no one living who could really miss it, even if there had been much to miss. But the story of Cahaba is echoed in hundreds of communities whose existence is threatened—not just hundreds of years ago but in this very moment: places that rely on the diminishing returns of punishment infrastructure, from incarceration to discrimination to servitude; families seeing their community institutions hollowed out, who were left without support in struggling times; people failed by a media wielded as a weapon, a media that refused to consider the moral dimensions of their work, who failed to engage with the three dimensions of their community.

But the fact that media is often weaponized does not preclude its potential as tool. This is what Cunningham seemed to be saying almost two hundred years ago: Media is how we get to the truth, but it is also a means to other ends. At its best, media creates community tasked with the ethic of care. What, I wonder, would that look like? For media to be treated by its handlers with care, as parents tasked with ushering in a world built on a value beyond shock, distraction, transactional engagement?

This is the task of civic media. It is not just presence but real intention—to see our communities as valuable and understand our role in maintaining them. A world where media does not merely exist and survive—but thrives, improves, imagines, expands, and transforms, facilitating accountability, trust, and, yes, care.

We Are More Than Bones

How Digital Spaces Are Shaping Black Futures

Rashida James-Saadiya

Rashida James-Saadiya (she/her) is the executive director of the Muslim Power Building Project and an independent scholar, artist, and cultural worker. Her work explores the intersections between resistance, collective care, and kinship among Black Muslim women in West Africa and the American South. Rashida's current project, Throwing Seeds, is a digital chronicle highlighting the Atlantic Ocean as a memory archive and a database for nonlinear narratives on repair and world-building.

In 2018, I began Betraying the Spectacle, a civic media project that relied on archival research, historical analysis, and ethnography to explore the intersections of identity, spirituality, and creative resistance in the lives of Black Muslim women in the American South. Through photographs, virtual story circles, poetics, and performance, I explored how Black Muslim women utilized creativity, affinity spaces, and collective action to combat patriarchy, racism, and gendered Islamophobia. The project was inspired by the scholarship of Dr. Barbara Christian, a pioneer in contemporary African American literary feminism, whose work expanded my understanding of how storytelling can be deployed as a medium for communication, survival, and future making and as a tool for undoing misconceptions in this context that Muslim women are subjects only but never experts on the complexities of their lives. As she so eloquently stated: "If Black women don't say who they are, other people will and say it badly for them."

Despite recent demographic shifts, the South is still very much a part of the Bible Belt, and the historical presence of Black Muslim women within its landscape is vast and complicated. To be a visible religious minority, a person of color, and a woman adds multiple layers of marginality. In addition, Western media continues to function as a tool of erasure, flattening Muslim women and reducing their bodies to a particular type of oppression that occurs exclusively within the "Muslim world" and never outside of it.

Statistical research shows that up to one-third of the US Muslim population is Black. Yet, issues of anti-Black racism, poverty, mass incarceration, and police brutality are rarely considered legitimate Muslim issues—creating a liminal space where Black Muslim women are simultaneously rendered invisible and perceived as dangerous due to enduring tropes that contribute to their continued marginalization. In preparation for this project, I put out a call for contributions within my network and quickly began collecting images and personal narratives from educators, creatives, activists, master gardeners, and community workers. Each story aided me in creating workshops on anti-Blackness and the historical role of religion and art in social justice movements, as well as talk spaces and virtual story circles on kinship and collective care. From academic presentations, panels, published

essays, and poetics, Betraying the Spectacle grew quickly, illuminating the importance of Black Muslim women reclaiming space to reorient conversations around race, spirituality, social injustice, and gender inequity.

And then a global pandemic happened, shifting everything.

Within a few months, the pandemic had interrupted the trappings of individualism. I did what is often necessary in times of tragedy: I sought community, emotional support, and a place to vent. Digital spaces became an uncurated, makeshift lifeline overflowing with COVID support groups, misinformation, conspiracy theories, books to read while social distancing, mutual aid initiatives, tips for preserving social connectedness, and musings on how to stay safe.

The concept of "safety" and performative digital bliss was complicated for Black women, who were placed in the middle of two pandemics: the outbreak of COVID-19 and the impact of systemic racism. Although the virus is not directly linked to race, it was especially destructive in Black communities, illustrating health inequities rooted in historic and ongoing social and economic injustices. The intersections of class, gender, health, and race collided, placing a particular strain on Black women given our disproportionate representation in front-line jobs that put us at a higher risk of contracting the virus. We were navigating increased caregiving demands, protests against police brutality, the uncertainty of economic security, and the arduous task of negotiating mental and physical wellness while reminding the world that our lives matter.

What has been understudied is how Black women acquired technological agency by being resourceful, innovative, and, most importantly, creative, as they used media to build a digital self-help society. Catherine Knight Steele, feminist scholar and author of *Digital Black Feminism*, asserts that how Black women create digital safe spaces and platforms for "intentional discourses of resistance is predicated upon a historically unique position of having to exist in multiple worlds and manipulate various technologies, and maximize resources."[1] In doing so, Black women make the internet a space for collaborative care and resistance and an affirming Black space, by decentering whiteness as the default internet identity.

The social positioning of Blackness requires Black women in particular to view technology as a new vision or tool for "addressing imbalances—between groups of people, but also between humans and their environment."[2] Black women navigate cyberspace in ways that far surpass the possibilities for it and, in doing so, create possibilities for themselves and others. Although "self-help" implies a focus on the individual, these networks, pages, sites, or groups are inherently participatory, offering members the opportunity to give and receive mutual support and collaborative care by sharing knowledge, lived experience, joy, dreams, and strategies to

address common issues. Self-help societies serve as an alternative public square where Black women exist in a liminal space with agency and time to imagine alternatives to current social and political realities and reclaim the importance of healing, kinship, pleasure, rest, and catharsis while facing the unknown.

However, after a few months, I abruptly severed my digital lifeline due to feeling bombarded by increased cyberbullying, xenophobia, trolling, sexual harassment, anti-Blackness, and "toxic positivity" posts instructing readers to suppress negative feelings and exist only in a state of positivity. The task of displaying an abundance of good vibes was outside my current reality and countered what I desired—a space to be fully human. I must admit that unplugging from cyberspace was restorative and brought much-needed clarity. For example, if I were to go beyond Zoom meetups and virtual affinity spaces, it would require a plan. Reestablishing my union with the internet meant thinking more deeply about what I wanted from the digital realm and what I was prepared to contribute or build if I could not find it. When I needed it most, a preordered book arrived, *Black Imagination: Black Voices on Black Futures*, an anthology inspired by an audio project created by conceptual artist Natasha Marin, who interviewed a diverse group of Black men, women, and youth using three questions: What is your origin story? How do you heal yourself? Describe/imagine a world where you are loved, safe, and valued. Part book and part archive, *Black Imagination* is a collection of testimonies and wisdom on how to heal yourself in uncertain times and envision a future and present in which humanness, Blackness, safety, and joy are not separated.

The internet is a place, and that place has largely been led by those who value the accumulation of capital over its users' access to safety, connection, or care.[3] Although a literary technology, *Black Imagination* swept through cyberspace, inspiring conversations on vision casting, Black joy, the correlation between self-care and community care, and how to make time for the act of imagining and building sustainable community spaces that favor relationships rather than transactions.

Imagining and believing in the possibilities of the future and present takes work. I struggled for days with the prompt from *Black Imagination*, "Imagine a world where you are safe." Being asked to simultaneously engage the past, survive in the present, and create an alternative future was arduous. Marin notes that it begins with unimagining what we believe is possible or have been taught about Blackness. The correlation between safety and wellness propelled me to start a monthly talk space via Zoom with creatives and cultural organizers who participated in Betraying the Spectacle. Over time, we invited others from within our

Imagining and believing in the possibilities of the future and present takes work.

networks, focusing on creative support, collaborative care, resource sharing, and the politics of Black joy. In essence, a space to engage the complexities and wonders of the everyday while investing in the present wellness of Black women, not as a response to exhaustion or oppression but as a birthright.

Technology is fascinating because it tells us so much about what has meaning for the people who create it—both how environments inspire ideas and how those ideas, in turn, can shape their environments.[4] During our monthly sessions, each participant was given the opportunity to grow an idea or root our time together by contributing a piece of art—poetry, short story, image, episode, podcast, music, and so on—that stretched their imagination and opinions about world making, media, and liberation. The multitude of resources, ideas, and inspiration gathered in this space led me to explore the possibilities of self-help societies and how Black women have utilized technology to create affinity spaces and ultimately inspired my current work Throwing Seeds, a digital chronicle and publication that highlights the Atlantic Ocean as a memory archive and site of diasporic consciousness in the lives of Black artists and cultural workers.

Over time, our digital support space became a community of African, Black American, and Afro-Caribbean folks. The killings of George Floyd and Breonna Taylor inspired conversations about how and why many Black Americans were leaving for countries like Ghana more than four hundred years after their ancestors were forcibly taken away. Others shared the physical, spiritual, and emotional toll of watching family members "taking the back way," a euphemism used in the Gambia to refer to the millions of people who risk their lives traveling across the Mediterranean Sea for economic opportunities in Europe, and musings about the urgency for Black creatives and thinkers to design digital spaces and practices to amplify underexplored histories and knowledge.

Is there a place in this physical world where Black people are safe? How do we envision and create digital and physical environments to explore the wisdom or ways of being of our ancestors before the interruption of slavery and colonization? These questions grounded my vision for Throwing Seeds, which pays homage to women who braided rice and other grains into their children's hair as a means of sustenance and survival during the Middle Passage. Their creativity and love in the midst of struggle and sorrow created an ecosystem of protection and resources that continue to nurture their descendants. The Atlantic Ocean is not simply a body of saltwater that covers one-fifth of the earth's surface. As Nigerian poet Daisy Odey defines it, "The bed of the Atlantic is an African cemetery; there is a lost continent there." So, how could the Atlantic ever be thought of as only water? I describe the Atlantic as a cosmic space that transcends geography, a living archive, a holder of

memory, a bridge that connects the past and the present, the ancestral world and the world of the living. For many, an origin story.

We are more than just the coding of genetic material, more than bones. We are walking stories, mirrors reflecting what is valued, carriers of society's politics, history, fears, hopes, victories, and failings. Equal parts gathering space, chronicle, and publication, Throwing Seeds will utilize art, literature, film, and storytelling to provoke conversations about navigating race, gender representation, spirituality, and the role of collective memory, imagination, and wisdom as cultural technologies illustrating who Black people are, have been, and are becoming as a politics of freedom, agency, and present making. This work is rooted in a long tradition of Black folks finding any means necessary to preserve their stories and dreams. Enslaved Africans recorded their experiences and memories through folktales told in secret and family trees documented in Bibles, while later generations saved family photos and heirlooms.

Inspired in part by the "digital garden" concept, my focus point is creating gathering space for Black memory and imagination, connecting Black women across time and space. Writer and designer Annika Hansteen-Izora defines "digital gardens" as virtual spaces tended to by a collective group of people with "seeds"—forms of digital media such as photos, art, videos, text—created with the intention of collective growth and sustainability. In this context, Black digital gardens are not imagined or designed to be magical utopias but instead are made up of "gardeners" who have settled into the ebb and flow of establishing protopias, "a state that is better today than yesterday."[5] I believe we need protopias, or alternative digital spaces for remembrance, hard questions, new ideas, and collective dreams that lead to community building and action offline. I am interested in stretching the digital landscape to hold, archive, and propel Black cultural memory, creativity, and the complexities of Blackness while refashioning the internet as a pathway to broaden empathy and collective moral responsibility.

This project centers itself within the challenges of navigating the many ways Black people globally are rendered inhuman and the recent focus on Black futures and Afrofuturism as a progressive form of envisioning that which does not yet exist but is also a rallying cry in response to structural racial violence. I believe the construction of Black digital spaces and cultural production should not be associated solely with the future but perhaps also with "post-present" memory, less futurism and more what are Black people across the diaspora experiencing right now and what do they need to thrive?

Reclaiming my relationship with the internet, reimagining cyberspace as a realm that requires wading through the mess to get to the good part, shifted

something in me. Perhaps it was discovering others who wanted humanness from the expansiveness of technology, who had a love-hate relationship with the interwebs but ultimately made peace with the unpleasant parts by building new worlds. Some examples are DEAR NOAH,[6] a visual time capsule and love letter to the next generation illustrating and documenting the worldwide civil rights movement of 2020 through the lens of Black women; Black Women of Print,[7] a digital homeplace initiated during the pandemic to promote the visibility of Black women printmakers via educational outreach to create a more equitable future within the discipline of printmaking; and The Nap Ministry, created by Tricia Hersey, who increased her digital efforts during the pandemic and loudly asked us all, "When will you realize that rest is also resistance?" Other examples of the wealth of insights, humor, spiritual reflections, history, action, and radical dreams that have grown across cyberspace are There Are Black People in the Future, a project that addresses systemic oppression of Black communities through space and time, and Somewhere Good, a social app that connects people and then fosters that connection in a group setting, across a diversity of interests—such as a birdwatching collective for people of color or an anti-capitalist book club. The rise of Black women using cyberspace to inspire collective healing, transformative relationships, abundance, creativity, and radical vision is not simply a trend but a seed.

Reclaiming my relationship with the internet shifted something in me.

I believe that cyberspace provides portals into other worlds, both real and imagined, that it can be used as a tool for counter-storytelling, reimagining, and liberation from a world of racial and gendered oppression. It is a pathway for radical vision and finding community across time and space. Through digital practice and cultural production, Black women have occupied digital spaces not reserved for their humanity, wisdom, ideas, joy, or vulnerability, reshaping cyberspace into more than an information space but also part of the sacred work of creating a new world.

Joining a long list of others who have committed themselves to filling in the gap via Throwing Seeds, my focus is to provide a platform for the Black diaspora to speak for themselves, publish work and art that interrogates memory and history, and center Black future making and present building, as well as to examine culture, religion, activism, joy, and liberation through a Black technoculture lens and the act of re-memory, which Toni Morrison defined as the act of reexamining the relation between ourselves and how we remember our individual and collective past, how that enters into our present, and how the past can serve either to repress or to reinvigorate our future—in essence, highlighting the complexities and wonders of each day through Black technoculture, the interweaving of technology, culture, self, and identity, and the intergenerational transmission of memory. In June 2021, I relocated with several Black creatives from the Betraying the Spectacle virtual group living in the American South. We left America to reconnect with the continent, each of us carrying memories of a place we had yet to see in search of a safe space to live and plant new roots. Suppose the ability to remember is a critical muscle. What happens when one seeks refuge from the impact of racial hierarchy by leaving memories behind in the hope that creating new memories, moments, and ways of being will have the power to address the scarring of history and the present day. Time spent living in Dakar, Senegal, shaped my perspective on literature, art, and affinity spaces as forms of technology. I see cyberspace as a space to explore how we hold memory in our bodies, live out Black joy, and map the connections between self-care and community care. This creates a digital ecosystem rooted in Black creativity, collaborative learning, action, dreaming, and liberation—a vast space for placemaking.

What is "placemaking" you might ask? In this context, it is the continual renewal of desacralized Black space into newly sacralized Black space through love and attention and community,[8] the act of finding or creating a space where one belongs and in that space learning to design a community care manifesto to meet the needs of the collective. Throughout history, Black women have pieced together spirituality, creativity, and ways of being to care for themselves, each other, and the communities they call home. My understanding of liberation and civic media

continues to evolve, but it rests on the need for connection and community. The pandemic arrived with many unexpected things, including time and the necessity to quickly learn how to navigate chaos and uncertainty. Finding digital refuge gave me the opportunity to listen to many visions of how Black people move forward and what it means to thrive and embody Black joy. The internet gave me the space to ask, Who will we be when the dust has settled and how will we get there together?

Notes

1 Catherine Knight Steele, *Digital Black Feminism* (New York University Press, 2021).
2 Florence Okoye, "Afrofuturism and Outsider Tech," *How We Get to Next*, February 2, 2016, https://www.howwegettonext.com/afrofuturism-and-outsider-tech/.
3 Annika Hansteen-Izora, "On Digital Gardens: Tending to Our Collective Multiplicity," *Deem Journal*, accessed July 23, 2023, https://www.deemjournal.com/stories/digital-gardens.
4 Okoye, "Afrofuturism and Outsider Tech."
5 Hansteen-Izora, "On Digital Gardens."
6 DEAR NOAH, accessed July 23, 2023, https://www.dearnoahproject.com/.
7 Black Women of Print, accessed July 23, 2023, https://www.blackwomenofprint.com/.
8 Alice Grandoit-Šutka and Nu Goteh, "Sacralized Space: Theaster Gates on the Practice of Placemaking," *Deem Journal*, accessed July 23, 2023, https://www.deemjournal.com/stories/theaster-gates.

Museum Curation as Care

Civic Media, Black History, and Communicating Afrofuturist Imaginings

Tyree Boyd-Pates

(in conversation with Sangita Shresthova)

Tyree Boyd-Pates (he/him) is a Los Angeles–based museum curator, professor, writer, speaker, activist, and historian who expounds on Black culture from a millennial vantage point and mobilizes communities of color through journalism, social media, education, and history.

I am a historian, museum curator, thinker, speaker, activist, author, and cultural consultant. I work to challenge power dynamics within traditional museum spaces and ensure that they include and center historically marginalized communities. I use civic media to bridge the gap between physical and digital spaces and make art and culture accessible to all audiences.

My civic media understanding began during my undergraduate studies in communications at Cal State University Bakersfield. There, I learned about Marshall McLuhan, a philosopher of communication theory who theorized that "the medium is the message." I wasn't aware of it at the time. Still, this theory became remarkably significant in my work as a communicator and museum curator because I began to understand that if the medium is just as important as its message, what messages are museums emitting, and how can they, as mediums, be used for inclusive purposes, especially for audiences of color, and specifically for African Americans, for liberatory purposes?

This realization would unfold after graduating from Temple University with my master's in Africology and African American studies. Wanting to use both degrees simultaneously, I utilized the internet as an organizing tool to share my expertise. After gaining popularity for amplifying the stories of activists involved in the Black Lives Matter movement on social media in Ferguson, Missouri, I gathered that the best way to use both degrees was to become a civic journalist. However, I soon realized that most journalists are not adequately compensated for their work. So instead, I brought my investigative, communication, and Black studies expertise to the classroom, teaching Africana studies at Cal State Dominguez Hills to first-year students where I understood the classroom's breadth and limitations for me, based on it as a medium.

Ultimately, I decided to pursue museum curation to reach a wider audience. As a newly minted museum curator and historian, I began to see my work as a political act because I was wielding institutional mediums for cultural purposes.

I soon learned that civic media, journalism, communications, and curation were powerful tools that can either uplift or denigrate communities of color, especially Black people. With the recognition of that power as a museum curator, I aim

to reclaim history through civic media, journalism, communications, and more recent omitted histories to form a path toward a brighter future for marginalized communities.

Museums Are Political Spaces

Museums serve a significant role beyond just being physical spaces for storing historical objects. They are also political spaces representing mainstream society's versions of progress and periodically even its regression. As a cisgender Black male museum professional, being in this field is a political act, primarily when only 5 percent of all museum curators identify as Black overall. Therefore, my presence as a museum professional is influential, and I can contribute to recentering history equitably by exerting that responsibility.

Museums have been a crucial part of my life since childhood. I still remember the first exhibit I can recall at the Los Angeles County Museum of Art (LACMA), where I saw Vincent van Gogh's retrospective, *Van Gogh's Van Goghs: Masterpieces from the Van Gogh Museum, Amsterdam*, when I was ten. Walking through the exhibit with my grandmother, I noticed the museum visitors fawning over Van Gogh's art. This experience taught me that art communicates with people and that you can understand the priorities of a society by observing this.

I also visited the California African American Museum (CAAM) with my grandmother, noticing essential similarities and differences between the two spaces. Black visitors experienced the same sense of intrigue and discovery, but inside this museum, Black people saw themselves portrayed with dignity and respect. This experience allowed me to see that Black communities receive recognition and honor very differently within society—specifically in their own culturally specific museums—compared with the art I saw when I visited LACMA as a young Black boy.

As I've progressed in age, I've realized that the seeds sown in my younger years through various experiences have equipped me to provide similar examples to young Black individuals hoping to see themselves in an elevated and dignified light. However, to achieve this, I had to educate myself on how to become a museum professional. Through volunteering and working at CAAM, I discovered that I could change the course of my community by replicating the same actions that caught my attention when I was merely ten years old.

Museum Curators Are World-Builders

Museum curators are world-builders, and as museum curators, we should focus on being people-centered and holding the stories and people whom the history and art are about. This can only be achieved when the lives of those people are adequately centered. One way to accomplish this is by using different futuristic modalities like Afrofuturism.

Being an Afrofuturist, I understand the importance of world-building in Afrofuturism. As a museum curator, I have curated exhibitions that allow Black people and communities in South Central Los Angeles and beyond to see themselves centered in an immersive space. Unfortunately, there aren't many other spaces outside of curated leisure spaces or events by Black people where Black folks can see themselves elevated. Therefore, I took on the responsibility as a curator at CAAM to world-build a historical account, retelling, or experience that was primarily immersive and built for Black museum visitors and patrons.

Museums need to be known for being equitable. Even the fact that there are ethnically specific museums is telling. For so long, white mainstream museums have locked out communities of color at large. Whenever there were exhibitions of communities of color within white mainstream museums, they were anthropological and extractive at best. Often, they veered into unacknowledged colonial plunder and displays of bounty by the holdings they possessed.

If museums hope to become more civic and people-centered, they must revisit why they were built, acknowledge and repair those fractures, and reassign who curates the objects in their galleries and holdings.

As a museum curator and historian, I preserve and present Black history and culture with care and respect. Being a Black man living in America, I use my personal experiences and identity to inform my work and represent not just myself but an entire community and its history within this context.

Within the museum field, this involves mediating discussions about the importance of Black histories that have been overlooked for generations. For example, I have previously worked on an exhibition about the foundational contributions of Black cowboys to the American public at the Autry Museum of the American West. Through this exhibition, I sought to unite different sides and encourage contemporary Black cowboys to negotiate a relationship with the institution while building rapport with the Black equestrian community in Los Angeles and advocating for the museum to recognize their contributions.

As a history curator, I fundamentally believe I am the guardian and caretaker of Black history and culture. I take my responsibility seriously and strive to deliver it to everyone else's doorstep.

Community Curation

As a museum curator, I firmly believe that community engagement is essential in museum curation across all types of institutions. I experienced notable success in this aspect, mainly while working with ethnic communities and museums.

For example, CAAM in South Los Angeles wanted to showcase the history of its community through its exhibits. However, I soon noticed that the most relevant stories were not found within the museum's holdings but were hidden in basements, attics, and churches. To tell these stories, the museum and curators like me had to rely on local outside experts and community archivists within Los Angeles's Black community to support the museum in gathering exhibition information, artifacts, and narratives to fill those gaps—therefore recentering omitted narratives.

This curatorial approach proved successful because our marginalized community felt included when invited to participate and had a stake in the project's success through their lived experience. As a result, the institution became more relevant. It decided to engage "with" the community and not "for" the community because it felt it would benefit from it. I've learned and expanded upon this museological approach called "Community Curation," or the radical inclusion and recentering of communities of color who are seldom involved in the museum curatorial decision-making processes.

I believe that this museological approach is radical in a field that has a legacy of colonialism, scientific racism, enslavement, rape, and plunder. However, it is not an impossible method, and it is a much-needed approach to reimagining museums futuristically. I believe that the museum field is primed and ready to address its involvement in the colonial process, and Community Curation as a theory could help significant museum reform efforts, building upon the repatriation of American Indigenous tribal ancestors' bodies and ancient bronze statues from West Africa back to the communities from which they came.

I think that museum protests and boycotts by visitors will ensue if museums don't recognize and reconcile these colonial histories. Community Curation is an adequate intervention that could finally open museums up to everyone through positive antiracist discourse and actions.

Museum Curation as Civic Media

For a civic media practitioner, museum curation is an excellent avenue to explore civic media. Our fellowship inherently follows an interdisciplinary approach. We understand that the medium is integral to the message, as the McLuhan theory always espoused. Our focus as practitioners is morally balanced between the

medium and the message we aim to convey because neither can be sacrificed when we deliver our projects. As practitioners, we bring that dedicated intensity to communicating our message, regardless of the medium we choose.

Currently, museum curation is one way I express my message, but I may pivot to another medium, like painting, in the next five to ten years. Regardless of the medium, I maintain the same specificity and intensity of my message. The beauty of civic media is that it accommodates interdisciplinary practitioners like me like no other field, especially those who use Afrofuturism to assist us in charting new courses of imagining societal possibilities.

All civic media practitioners share a common thread: We bring passion and intensity to conveying our message. We find inspiration in the unexpected, and the field thrives on this. Who knows what the future holds? In twenty years, the definition of civic media may evolve, but our commitment to conveying impactful messages will always endure.

The Seven Steps of Planning an Exhibit

The process of planning an exhibit for museum curators is quite extensive. It involves seven official steps.

The first step in curating an exhibition that seeks originality is to assert a solid thesis and the exhibition's ability to defend it. Everything is rooted in the thesis; for example, the sky is blue because of *x* reason.

Second, the curator aggregates and delves into scholarly research to substantiate their curatorial thesis.

Third, the curator explores the objects to substantiate their thesis with the archive and ephemera. These objects are either in the museum's permanent collection or housed elsewhere, typically within the community.

Fourth, the curator writes and synthesizes the information for the texts and objects within the exhibit.

Fifth, with all this writing, the curator works with the exhibition supervisor to design the physical space.

Sixth, the curator works on installing the exhibition. This is when the team and I bring everything into the space.

The seventh and final step is opening and inviting all players involved and the community, who will validate and amplify the power of the curator's thesis.

Our Civic Media

Portraying My Community Through My Lens

SHAN Wallace

(with Pratik Nyaupane from an interview by Javier Alcantara)

SHAN Wallace (she/her) is a nomadic award-winning interdisciplinary artist, archivist, and image maker from Baltimore. SHAN uses a range of mediums to weave narratives and imagine new stories. Rooted in image-making techniques such as photography, film, and collage, as well as in situ installations, these mediums serve as the foundation of her artistic practice. SHAN's work is in both public and private collections across the United States. She has exhibited work internationally in galleries and museums, including the Baltimore Museum of Art and the Annenberg Space for Photography in Los Angeles. SHAN lives and works in many spaces between Brooklyn and Baltimore.

I grew up as a Black child in Baltimore during the '90s, and I've come to understand that rejecting the dominant narratives about Black people—especially in Baltimore—requires a unique strength, resilience, and self-love. Far too often, harmful and untruthful narratives are pushed by those who don't look like us, telling a distorted, one-sided story of our communities. Television shows such as *The Wire*, along with mainstream media coverage, frequently present negative, misleading portrayals of where I'm from. These dominant narratives have had a long-lasting impact, creating a stigma that shapes how we are often viewed by others and each other. Having been born here and having witnessed firsthand the effects of these stereotypes, I feel a deep responsibility to document my city with care and attentiveness and to stay committed to sharing our stories. Many of us face erasure, and so my work, in whatever form it takes, is about ensuring that we are the authors of our own narratives. My role in this creative space is to make images that celebrate us, that allow us to take pride in who we are, and to show many sides of the story.

Image Maker

As an artist, my goal is to choose the medium that best supports the story I want to tell. As a photographer, my process is like water: shapeless and formless. Fluidity is a key part to my process, allowing me to stay grounded during changes and pivots.

My work is never just about me. I am a reflection of my people and an extension of my community. When I photograph people, I make sure to give them copies of the images; it's one of my principles and a way to share authorship over the work. I want these copies to advocate for the importance of archives and the power of the images shaping our collective history. The people I photograph aren't just subjects; they become collaborators in this work. Often, those I photograph become family, supporters, and active participants in the ongoing collection of our stories.

I never anticipated how life-changing this work would be for me and the city I love. I've received overwhelming support from Baltimore. From the simple act of giving people copies of photographs, I've had people pray for me, pray *with* me, and genuinely wish me well. These are rewards that you can't put a price on. But it's

those affirmations that remind me, *I'm doing something that has a real impact on people's lives*. That means everything to me and is why I continue to do this work. It's why I always keep Baltimore in my heart.

Summer of George Floyd

After George Floyd's murder in the summer of 2020, I realized just how shut out many of us were from mainstream media. I and many other journalists, photographers, graphic designers, and filmmakers—predominantly Black, Indigenous, Latino, and other people of color—were flooded with work and assignments that were disguised as a genuine interest in our work, but ultimately they were just an opportunity for many of these institutions to reckon with and work through their guilt of excluding us and many before us. I secured more commercial work in three months than I had in the previous five years.

It was a real wake-up call to know that before that, our work was on people's vision boards and being referenced, but we weren't being hired. It was clear we were intentionally being overlooked and ignored despite being qualified and talented. Quickly the momentum for that racial reckoning faded, the work slowed down and then disappeared, and we went back to being an afterthought and unhired.

Imagining Civic Media

There is this deep divide when the media producers don't care about the people and the people no longer trust the media. Civic media is breaking free from the traditional ecosystem that has long controlled societal narratives. Simply put, we're challenging that ecosystem and status quo.

I see my work as civic media. While traditional media is controlled by massive corporations and billionaires whose priorities are making profits and pushing specific narratives, civic media prioritizes an equitable and accountable future for media that emphasizes community involvement, dialogue, and democratic participation.

I believe civic media is the future of media, with resistance at its core. It's a deliberate alternative approach. It's media created by us and for us, with "us" being an inclusive term meaning everyone has a voice and role. It's like basketball: Everyone has a position and for the team to succeed, everyone must contribute. Civic media invites the community to steer the direction and shape the message.

Civic media holds the potential to reshape the way we receive and engage with information. It empowers us with tools to make decisions and cultivate rituals and practices that improve our lives. It's about creating tools within media that serve the people, not the powerful.

I believe civic media is the future of media, with resistance at its core.

How Big Does Civic Media Need to Be?

AX Mina

AX Mina (she/they) is an author, artist, and filmmaker. AX has led exhibitions in spaces such as the Victoria and Albert Museum, the Mozilla Festival Artist Open Studios (curated by the V&A Museum and Tate Modern), and the Museum of the Moving Image. She is the author of *Memes to Movements: How the World's Most Viral Media Is Changing Social Protest and Power* and a coauthor of *The Hanmoji Handbook: Your Guide to the Chinese Language Through Emoji*.

"Thank you for that," a student said. "I really needed that time." We had just finished a yoga class I'd taught—an online class of just four students, all friends of mine willing to take a chance on a new yoga teacher. It was one of my first yin yoga classes since being certified to teach yoga, and I was nervous. I prepared a routine that involved long, slow holds of popular poses like *balasana* (child's pose) and *matsyasana* (fish pose), and I combined it with poetry from Kahlil Gibran, one of my favorite poets.

"The river cannot go back," he wrote. "Nobody can go back."

In the before times, that is, before COVID-19, my vision of civic media was shaped by scale. My initial explorations of civic media included software, like the development of online fact-checking and translation tools; discussion on platforms like Twitter, where a baseline level of "success" included thousands, if not tens or hundreds of thousands, of followers; and media for social movements that reached the front pages of newspaper and major news broadcasts.

Then came COVID, and my world, like the world of so many people, shrank. The stage talks transitioned into Zoom talks—just as many people, but nowhere near the high-energy vibe of speaking in front of a crowd—and social media lacked the same kind of oomph without in-person gatherings to bolster them.

After the 2021 Atlanta shootings in which a gunman killed eight people, six of whom were women of Asian descent, artist Jason Li and I held space for members of the Asian diaspora to grieve. In-person gatherings were still out of the question. We didn't want to do it on Zoom, which felt too clinical and associated with work. Instead, we built on top of LIFELIKE, an open-source, virtual world with 8-bit-like aesthetics, developed by Molleindustria. People could choose a name and avatar and move their figure around a space we designed with soothing music.

About twelve people showed up, sharing reflections and lighting digital candles. Because no video was involved, the platform became an important medium for grief, as no one needed to show their faces or feel the need to perform. They could express themselves with their avatars' gestures and written comments. It was one of the most powerful, moving experiences of my life, and very few people knew about it. It was small. We didn't advertise it much or write a big mission statement. That was the point.

I wrote an essay called "Make Space for Grieving: How Can Communities Grieve in a Time of Social Distancing?" on my Medium page in March 2021.[1] It was just a year after the WHO declared the COVID-19 pandemic, but for me it felt like a completely different life.

Today, COVID-19 still makes it difficult for us to come together in the same way. A dear friend of mine has been navigating grief this past year, and I've not had a single opportunity to hug them or take them out to dinner or share space with them. Instead, we text regularly, talk on the phone, and trade photos and videos on occasion. One time, they sent me a picture of themselves, and I realized I hadn't seen their face in over a year.

"You look so sad," I said.

"I am," they said.

They're not the only friend I've said this to after they sent me a recent selfie. Around the world, friends whom I used to see regularly now navigate their grief in much smaller communities than they might have before COVID-19. Some of them navigate their grief entirely alone.

One of the challenges of scale is that the numbers belie the transformation. It's easy to see a YouTube video of a documentary getting thousands of views, but what does it mean? How did it affect people?

One of the early rules of internet culture is the 1-9-90 rule: 90 percent of community members consume content, another 9 percent contribute or edit the content, and only 1 percent actually generate new content. It's a close cousin to the Pareto principle, which holds that 20 percent of contributors will generate 80 percent of the results, whether in online activity, global economics, or civics (the principle is named after Italian sociologist Vilfredo Pareto's observation that 80 percent of Italy's land was owned by 20 percent of the population).

What the 1-9-90 rule doesn't show is what it means to be the 90 percent who consume content. It's easy to assume that's all they do—consume—but every act of consumption contains the seeds of transformation. Why did they consume the media? What did they learn? What series of thoughts emerged? In a world of metrics, there's no way to know. At scale, we get a few comments in the comment threads, but no sense of the long-term shift in knowledge and consciousness that civic media has the potential to enable.

ooo

"The latest episode of your podcast brought me to tears," a friend messaged me after listening to *Five and Nine*, a podcast about magic, work, and economic justice that I cofounded toward the latter part of 2022, as the world was slowly reemerging from COVID lockdowns. Up until that point, my media practice had focused a lot on intellectual insights, on using reason to make the best argument. But I was struck by this response—tears.

"Tears are a form of insight too," a colleague told me. "Sometimes, they're even more insightful, because it means the person felt it deeply."

A few hundred people listen to our episodes, slowly; I watch the numbers tick up over the course of months after a given release, and the emails roll in over that same time frame, if they do at all. One listener told me she waits to tune in to episodes only during long flights but that when she does, she takes a lot of notes.

Apparently this is typical for small, indie podcasts. Unlike social media and television, they're often consumed slowly, and the numbers are much smaller. While some podcasts go viral and gain a ton of views right away, most move slowly—according to some online benchmarks, having some one hundred listeners in seven days means your show is already in the top 25 percent of podcasts. Your podcast is above average with a little over thirty listeners in a week.[2]

But listening to a podcast is so different from watching a TikTok video. Yes, even simple short video posts might get thousands of views, but the type of energy given to a podcast is different. Someone has dedicated some thirty minutes of their life to listening to a conversation with limited visual stimuli. One 2022 study correlated podcast listening with people having a sense of meaning in life, openness to learning, and a general sense of curiosity.[3] There might not be a lot of visible metrics with podcasting, but something else is going on that's worth celebrating.

Is it civic media if you only reach one or two people? What about a few dozen? The very word "civic," coming from the Latin *civis*, or citizen, implies the scale of a city or empire. But it can also just mean that: a single citizen, floating out there in the world with their earbuds on a subway platform as they tune in to your work. Maybe they cry, maybe they get bored, maybe they take notes. Either way, they've given time and a private moment, and we have no metrics to capture that experience.

As I emerge from the COVID-19 pandemic, I've started wondering if the primacy we give to scale distracts us from other forms of impact.

"Our research and that of other scientists suggest that activation of the vagus nerve is associated with feelings of caretaking and the ethical intuition that humans from different social groups (even adversarial ones) share a common humanity," observed social scientist Dacher Keltner in *Scientific American*.[4] "People who have high vagus nerve activation in a resting state, we have found,

are prone to feeling emotions that promote altruism—compassion, gratitude, love and happiness."

In his book, *Awe: The New Science of Everyday Wonder and How It Can Transform Your Life*, Keltner notes that the emotion of awe in particular activates the vagus nerve in a way that helps us see our common humanity. Awe can come from seeing a mountain vista, watching a baby being born, or experiencing a moving piece of art. Or, I might add, even consuming a particularly effective form of civic media.

The Afrofuturist Ytasha Womack has pointed out that imagination is the process by which we envision alternative futures and have agency around the world we live in. "It's not just pure expression. It's not just a mode of inspiration. It does ultimately create levels of agency, where people feel that they can shape the world around them," she explained during a talk at the Sonic Acts Festival in Amsterdam.[5] "The imagination is important. The imagination is a lifeline. The imagination is an extension of the resilience of the human spirit."

The imagination is an extension of the resilience of the human spirit.

—YTASHA WOMACK

In the context of civic media, what both Keltner and Womack get at is the internal process of civic media, whether consuming, creating, or engaging with it. And while internal processes can happen at scale—Womack's video, for example, received over fifty thousand views as of press time, and Keltner is a best-selling author—these processes become more obvious, more potent, more visible at smaller scales. It's easier to describe and understand and engage with them, perhaps because it's easier to know they happened.

The point, of course, is not that we should disregard large-scale civic media projects. Rather, by articulating the value of small acts of civic media, we might start to think about other ways to measure and evaluate the role of civic media to begin with. In the face of all the massive protest movements of the twenty-first century, it's natural to ask what's changed. Sometimes there's no obvious policy shift or dictator toppled or border redrawn. Sometimes it looks like nothing at all has happened. But that's an outsider's perspective. The media people make to challenge norms in society percolate through society, slowly, until one day, a dreamy Occupy Wall Street slogan—Forgive Student Debt—becomes an actual federal policy battle over a decade later. It's messy, of course, as the battle continues to move on as of press time, but a decade ago it felt like the stuff of the imagination.

Journalist and researcher Clare Cook argued that sometimes the point of civic media is *not* to scale. She observes that civic media should be seen as having not just economic value but *social value*:

> This means going beyond a view of economic value that simply accounts for what we can exchange between one another, and the bottom-line cost. It asks, instead, what it is that people regard as meaningful in their lives, and how this can be articulated and represented in a diverse, inclusive, creative, democratic, socially just and joyous interplay of different types of media. It is through the lens of community and civic media—as social value media—that we are able to tell our own stories in our own words, about those things that matter to us, and which will improve our lives and our wellbeing.[6]

In the summer of 2021, I ventured out into Ernest E. Debs Regional Park in Los Angeles's Highland Park neighborhood. The Golden Dome School, a community dedicated to mysticism and the arts, was hosting their annual Resurrection of Care. A few dozen people showed up, and I was one of them.

Civic media should be seen as having not just economic value but *social value.*

The event had started in galleries and art festivals to reconnect people with the earth during a time of extraction. In 2020, it went online, and in 2021, it was outdoors. Participants circled the lake, carrying banners and playing music, and it was so odd to be around people again. At one point, a wailing broke out. With my emotions still balled up during lockdown—we all did what we needed to do to survive—I wasn't able to let out tears, but the ceremony did it for me.

As I wrote in my review of the performance in *Hyperallergic* in 2023,[7] the artists captured "the grief of living through the harrowing events of the pandemic and the wildfires in California in the summer of 2021. The performance offered a sense of healing and release during this catastrophic time." I wrote my brief review two years later, long after I'd seen the piece and documented it and spent time alone by the lake trying to make sense of all the feelings swirling inside me. It took me two years to internalize and understand the Golden Dome School's message of care, to make sense of what it had done for me.

As Gibran reminded me, the river of twenty-first-century crisis keeps floating along, and there is no way to go back. The school's performance was civic media writ small—with large transformations that continue to influence my own relationship with the earth. And in being small, it taught me something new—about myself, the world, and why we produce civic media at all.

Notes

1 AX Mina, "Make Space for Grieving: How Can Communities Grieve in a Time of Social Distancing?" Medium, March 18, 2021, https://anxiaomina.medium.com/make-space-for-grieving-53e69b619c4b.

2 "Average Podcast Downloads: Podcast Measurement and Growth," The Podcast Host, accessed August 3, 2023, https://www.thepodcasthost.com/planning/whats-a-good-number-of-downloads-for-a-podcast/.

3 Stephanie J. Tobin and Rosanna E. Guadagno, "Why People Listen: Motivations and Outcomes of Podcast Listening," PLoS One 17, no. 4 (April 6, 2022): e0265806, https://www.ncbi.nlm.nih.gov/pmc/articles/PMC8985929/.

4 Quoted in David DiSalvo, "Forget Survival of the Fittest: It Is Kindness That Counts," *Scientific American*, September 1, 2009, https://www.scientificamerican.com/article/forget-survival-of-the-fittest/.

5 Ytasha Womack, "Afrofuturism: Imagination and Humanity," video filmed February 26, 2017, at Sonic Acts Festival, Amsterdam, Netherlands, https://www.youtube.com/watch?v=xlF90sXVfKk.

6 Clare Cook, "When the Goal Is Not to Scale: How Can Civic and Community Media Be More Resilient?," Medium, October 18, 2019, https://clare-cook.medium.com/when-the-goal-is-not-to-scale-how-can-civic-and-community-media-be-more-resilient-4879089caf9c.

7 AX Mina, "Los Angeles Artists Find Community in Mysticism," *Hyperallergic*, July 28, 2023, https://hyperallergic.com/835571/los-angeles-artists-find-community-in-mysticism/.

Acknowledgments

First and foremost, thank you to all of the Civic Media fellows who have participated in our program, whether as a member of a cohort or as a mentor in the community, and shared their journeys with fellow travelers: Tanzila Ahmed, Maytha Alhassen, Derrick N. Ashong, Susu Attar, Marya Bangee, Amelia Barlow, Ahmed Best, BC Biermann, Jackson Bird, Danielle Blunt, Tyree Boyd-Pates, Ava Bromberg, Jamira Burley, Ingrid Burrington, Ben Caldwell, Charlene Carruthers, Ann Chen, Tanya DePass, Martha Diaz, Sue Ding, D'Lo, Crystal Echohawk, Arianne Edmonds, Mohammed El-Kurd, Eve Ewing, Carla Fernandez, Quetzal Flores, Niki Franco, Erin Fredman, Sofía Gallisá Muriente, Rae Garringer, Ifat Gazia, Nadege Green, Arshia Haq, Essence Harden, Sydette Harry, Set Hernandez, Elise Hu, Akilah Hughes, Rashida James-Saadiya, Jason Fitzroy Jeffers, Mary Jirmanus Saba, Jamal Jordan, Adrienne Keene, Raina Kumra Gardiner, Bryan C. Lee Jr., Nia Lee, Daniel Alejandro Leon-Davis, Erik Loyer, Ash Lukashevsky, Mari Mari Narváez, Terry Marshall, Kenya Miles, Jamel Mims, AX Mina, Darnell Moore, Justino Mora, Doris Muñoz, Yasmin Naboa, Diana Nucera, Genevieve Erin O'Brien, Kara Oehler, Anshantia Oso, Latoya Peterson, Amber J. Phillips, Harper Reed, Josie Duffy Rice, Jennifer S. Roberts, Jeff Severns Guntzel, Paisley Smith, Lissa Soep, Fresco Steez, Megan Stielstra, Dexter Thomas, Noy Thrupkaew, Magalis Videaux, SHAN Wallace, Xiaowei R. Wang, Sarah Weissman, Paige Wood, J Wortham, Anu Yadav, Jeff Yang, and Qianqian Ye.

We would like to extend our deepest thanks to Michelle Zenarosa, whose role as community lead from 2019 to 2022 was essential in shaping the programming and infrastructure for this community. Michelle's leadership in organizing programs, leading sessions, and contributing to the development of so many aspects of the initiative was instrumental. Michelle, your dedication to participatory practice and your influence on the ethos of the program have left an indelible mark, and we are profoundly grateful for your contributions.

We are greatly appreciative of the amazingly generative partnership we've had with Jennifer Humke, from cocreating the initial concept of the Civic Media Fellowship through its launch and evolution and into this next iteration. We could not have had more thoughtful, respectful, or committed collaborators on both the

fellowship and this book than you and your amazing colleagues at the the John D. and Catherine T. MacArthur Foundation, most notably Kathy Im and the rest of the Journalism & Media Team, Eric Sears, and John Palfrey.

To Megan Stielstra, we have been beyond fortunate to have had you in this community as a fellow, as a generous mentor and cheerleader to all the writers within it, and finally as an editor and champion of this book—thank you for bringing this work to the amazing team at Northwestern University Press and for your patience with us and our dedication to a participatory process and all that entailed.

We would like to extend our heartfelt thanks to Paul Mihailidis and Henry Jenkins for taking the time to read the manuscript of *We Are Civic Media* and providing invaluable feedback. Your thoughtful insights have greatly influenced this work.

We would like to express our deep gratitude to the graduate students at USC who worked alongside us over the years, conducting interviews with fellows, helping to shape the direction of this initiative, and contributing as integral members of our team. Cerianne Robertson, Javier Alcantara, Ally Arrieta, and Rogelio Lopez—your scholarship, dedication, insights, and collaboration have been invaluable throughout this process. Thank you for your commitment and for being an essential part of this journey.

Our staff and faculty colleagues at the Annenberg School for Communication and Journalism and across USC have been enduring supporters of the fellowship and all the work we do at the Annenberg Innovation Lab. In ways large and small, your guidance, enthusiasm, and support have been fundamental to our success.

There are, of course, so many other people who contributed to the creation of this book, from guest speakers, fellow nominators, and applicants who helped make the program what it is, to mentors, family, and friends who inspired, guided, and encouraged us to share our ideas. While writing (or a fellowship, for that matter) can be a solitary practice, we sought to make the process participatory and collaborative, which while somewhat complicated, was quite wonderful. That said, we note that any incongruities remain entirely our own, and we very much look forward to learning from them—together—as the static page gives way to an interactive dialogue.

For more background, context, resources, kudos, and inspiration for your own civic media practice, see wearecivicmedia.org.

About the Editors

Sangita Shresthova (she/her) is a writer, thinker, and practitioner whose recent publications include three coauthored books: *Practicing Futures: The Civic Imagination Action Handbook*, *Transformative Media Pedagogies*, and *Popular Culture and the Civic Imagination: Case Studies of Creative Social Change*. Sangita is the associate research professor of communication and director of the Civic Paths Group based at the University of Southern California. A Czech Nepalese child of the final years of the Cold War, Sangita grew up between Prague and Kathmandu; her childhood was shaped by hostile visa policies and travel restrictions, which reinforced her lifelong commitments to social justice and change.

Dan Sinker (he/him) is a journalist, multimedia artist, and program designer. He founded the influential magazine *Punk Planet* in 1994 when he was just nineteen years old and chronicled underground music, art, and politics for thirteen years. He was a JSK Fellow at Stanford University in 2007 and went on to found the journalism nonprofit OpenNews in 2011. Dan cohosts the long-running current events podcast *Says Who* and is a frequent contributor to *Esquire* magazine; he has also written for *The Atlantic*, *Slate*, and *The New York Times*. He joined the Civic Media Fellowship team in 2019 and lives just outside Chicago.

Pratik Nyaupane (he/him) is a PhD candidate at USC Annenberg, where he researches the cultures of datafication, perceptions of surveillance technologies, and digitization of public and civic life. His work investigates the opportunities and tensions of digital technologies and media as we seek to build more just, safe, and equitable futures. Having spent his early childhood in New Zealand and Nepal, Pratik grew up in Arizona, calling the sunny desert his home. Through his lived experience, he explores the practices of citizenship, migration, and borders, and how digital technologies have an impact on political and cultural processes.

Sophie Madej (she/her) has helped to implement and manage the Civic Media Fellowship from its inception. She is the program administrator at USC's Annenberg Innovation Lab and was previously knowledge manager for the Institute for Learning, a project at the University of Pittsburgh's Learning Research and Development Center.

Colin M. Maclay (he/him) specializes in the interaction of innovation and change with media, technology, and culture. A hacker of universities and committed collaborator, Colin bridges scholarship, practice, disciplines, and sectors. He has worked globally on topics including democracy, sustainability, entrepreneurship, and learning. As research professor of communication at USC, he directs the Annenberg Innovation Lab, Civic Media Fellowship, Presidential Sustainability Solutions Fellowship, Arts & Climate Collective, and Media As Socio-Technical Systems (MASTS). Colin founded Harvard Business School's Digital Initiative, managed Harvard's Berkman Klein Center for Internet & Society, and cofounded the Global Network Initiative.

ANNENBERG INNOVATION LAB

The Annenberg Innovation Lab (AnnLab) seeks to understand and shape social transformation through a mix of discovery, learning, and engagement. Committed to helping media and technology work for—not against—us, AnnLab explores the intersections of culture, community, participation, organizations, and policy in the context of a dynamic, digital, networked, and media-rich environment. We traverse disciplines, sectors, and communities at the University of Southern California and beyond to unite diverse scholars, practitioners, and organizations. We create and share media, technology, tools, and resources, endeavoring to work collaboratively and in the open and to invite others into the process to test and build upon our insights. Read more at http://www.annenberglab.org.

The USC AnnLab Civic Media Fellowship began with and continues to enjoy funding from the John D. and Catherine T. MacArthur Foundation. The Civic Media Fellowship is a program for artists, organizers, makers, storytellers, and others who use media and technology with participatory practices that advance social progress in ways that defy easy categorization and who want to invest in learning with and from each other, exploring new modes of expression and otherwise pushing their practice into unexpected places. The founding cohort launched in January 2019, followed by four subsequent cohorts in September of 2019, 2020, 2021, and 2022 (as of press time). Cohort sizes have ranged from nine to sixteen fellows, who receive a modest stipend and participate in weekly meetings online for nine months. Read more at http://www.civicmediafellowship.org/.